Revealed Comparative Advantage and Gravity Model Analysis of Trade Patterns and Regional Economic Integration

Published by
ACADEMIC FOUNDATION
in association with

The Indian Econometric Society (TIES)

ABOUT THE AUTHOR:

Amita Batra is Professor of Economics in the Centre for South Asian Studies, School of International Studies, Jawaharlal Nehru University (JNU), New Delhi. She was the first holder of the ICCR professorial chair in Contemporary Indian Studies at the Centre for South Asian Studies and Edinburgh-India Institute, University of Edinburgh, Edinburgh, UK during January-May 2013. She has worked extensively in the area of regional economic integration with a focus on Asia and her latest book on the subject is *Regional Economic Integration in South Asia: Trapped in Conflict?* (London: Routledge, 2012). Prof Batra holds an MA, MPhil and PhD in Economics from the Delhi School of Economics, University of Delhi, Delhi.

TIES Golden Jubilee Monograph Series-1

Revealed Comparative Advantage and Gravity Model Analysis of Trade Patterns and Regional Economic Integration

Empirical Evidence in the Indian Context

Amita Batra

ACADEMIC FOUNDATION
NEW DELHI

www.academicfoundation.org

First published in 2016
by

ACADEMIC FOUNDATION
4772-73 / 23 Bharat Ram Road, (23 Ansari Road),
Darya Ganj, New Delhi - 110 002 (India).
Phones : 23245001 / 02 / 03 / 04.
Fax : +91-11-23245005.
E-mail : books@academicfoundation.com
www.academicfoundation.org

in association with the
The Indian Econometric Society (TIES).

Disclaimer:
The findings/views/opinions expressed in this book are solely those of the author and do not necessarily reflect the views of the publisher.

Cataloging in Publication Data--DK
Courtesy: D.K. Agencies (P) Ltd. <docinfo@dkagencies.com>

Batra, Amita, author.
Revealed comparative advantage and gravity model analysis of trade patterns and regional economic integration : empirical evidence in the Indian context / Amita Batra.
pages cm
Includes bibliographical references.
ISBN 9789332703384

1. India--Commercial policy. 2. Comparative advantage (International trade) 3. Gravity model of international trade. I. Title.

HF1589.B38 2016 DDC 382.30954 23

Typeset, printed and bound by The Book Mint, New Delhi.
www.thebookmint.in

CONTENTS

LIST OF TABLES

Foreword

The Indian Econometric Society Trust, (TIES Trust) in association with The Indian Econometric Society, (TIES), launched the programme of publishing short monographs on select themes, as part of the Golden Jubilee Celebrations of the TIES. It is desired that these monographs would contain, among others, literature survey, critical reflections on the methodology, some empirical results, policy inferences, if any, as also an inventory of topics for further research. In view of these contents, the monographs are expected to be good publications, useful to the teaching professionals and researchers in Econometrics. The size of the monographs is prescribed to be around 100-150 pages, so that they could be easily carried to class rooms and conference venues.

We have identified a number of distinguished scholarsand requested them to prepare good monographs for publication in this Monograph Series.

Though started as part of the Golden Jubilee Year Celebrations, this programme is expected to continue as a regular programme of publications, in the service of the professional community of Econometrics. The monographs would be captioned as "TIES Golden Jubilee Monograph Series".

We subject the drafts of the monographs to peer review, to ensure that they are of high quality and that they fulfil the objectives of being useful aides to the teachers and the researchers in the profession.

We are pleased to bring out this first monograph in this series, entitled, "Revealed Comparative Advantage and Gravity Model Analysis of Trade Patterns and Regional Economic Integration: Empirical Evidence in the Indian Context", by Amita Batra, Professor, Jawaharlal Nehru University, New Delhi.

This monograph provides a useful survey of the literature, on the theme of "revealed comparative advantage" and on the "gravity models of trade analysis". It also contains insightful empirical results of applied work done by the author, along with some useful policy inferences.

We are pleased to announce that there are a number of monographs in the pipeline and we hope to bring them out in the next few months.

We would like to appeal to the scholars of the econometrics profession to come forward to take up the responsibility of producing good and useful monographs on the themes that are relevant to the teaching and research profession.

We would like express our appreciation of the valuable services being provided by the Academic Foundation in publishing and widely circulating the TIES Monographs.

This monograph has been carefully vetted by the editorial committee. We are grateful to the committee members. We express our appreciation and gratitude to Prof PamiDua, President, TIES, for her valuable support and guidance.We are also grateful to Dr N.R. Bhanumurthy, Secretary TIES, for his valuable spadework in carefully implementing this programme of monograph publications.

Suggestions for improving the quality and usefulness of this programme are welcome. It is proposed to make, in due course of time, the e-publications of the monographs for the benefit of the scholars in India and abroad.

Prof V.R.Panchamukhi and Prof K.L. Krishna
General Editors of "TIES Golden Jubilee Monograph Series"

1

Introduction

India made an extensive effort to liberalise its economy through systemic reforms initiated in 1991. As part of this process, trade and investment liberalisation involved increased exposure to competitive pressures and technology transfers that, it is expected, have led to a restructuring of India's comparative advantage in the global economy. Also, as India's trade integration with the global economy increased, trends of trade with the Asian economies, in particular China, became evident. The process is part of an overall trade strategy that starting with unilateralism and multilateralism has progressed to gradually encompass regionalism. While the progress of regionalism within South Asia has been formalised through economic instruments of SAPTA[1] followed by SAFTA,[2] India's participation in the larger context of Asian regionalism has been through Pan Asian configurations like the East Asia Summit. In case of South Asia, the pace of regionalism has been slow on account of high tariffs, NTBs (non-tariff barriers) political factors and historical rivalries among member nations. Asian integration has moved at a relatively faster pace with participation from India, through formulation of new age FTAs (free trade agreements) and comprehensive economic partnerships at the bilateral and plurilateral levels.

India's trade integration at the global and regional level has often been compared with China. In the context it needs to be recognised that China and India are not just similar in size but also in factor endowments. Increased trade integration of China over the past few years is likely to have contributed to a shift in comparative advantage in labour intensive manufactures in the world market. This development

1. SAARC Preferential Trading Arrangement.
2. South Asian Free Trade Area.

is pertinent to India, and it is important therefore, to explore the extent of similarity in the patterns of comparative advantage for the two economies and the implications, if any, of the same for regional integration processes in Asia.

Given these developments, this monograph is an attempt to analyse the pattern and dynamism in the structure of India's comparative advantage and India's bilateral trade patterns and potentials as captured by the gravity model. The analysis is undertaken in the overall context of regional economic integration in Asia with due recognition of the implications of preferential trade agreements (including FTAs) signed or implemented by India. These issues are analysed from the Indian perspective in terms of the available evidence, empirical analysis and relevant policy formulations over the last two decades.

The analysis presented in this monograph draws on existing research and published papers on the issues under discussion. The analysis is undertaken mainly with respect to merchandise trade. Studies on India's RCA (revealed comparative advantage) in trade in services or gravity model based analysis of the services trade in the Indian context are limited. In general, the literature on trade in services is yet confounded by and grappling with deficiencies in data. Studies using the concept of RCA or gravity model that have, as part of a global or developing country perspective, included India in the analysis are discussed in relevant sections of the monograph.

The monograph proceeds as follows. The next section presents a brief theoretical background to broadly contextualise the issues under consideration against some relevant trade theory constructs. Even while the theoretical aspects to the extent that they are pertinent are discussed it is to be realised that the distance between theory and application and even more policymaking is huge. The different sections in this monograph in a way bring to the fore the many dimensions of this spectrum. Theoretical background is followed by a brief review of India's integration with the global economy individually, and in a comparative framework with China. This is followed by a detailed discussion of each issue with specific reference to its theoretical evolution, measurement, estimation methodologies and available empirical evidence in the Indian context. At some points, as indicated above, a comparative analysis with the Chinese economy has been presented.

1.1 Theoretical Background

The two main theories of trade based on comparative advantage are the Ricardian theory and the Heckscher-Ohlin (H-O) theory. Ricardo proposed the idea of free trade as a means to achieve productive efficiency at a global level based on the argument of cost calculations in terms of labour hours, treated as single homogeneous input with production in a two commodity world being subject to constant costs. Comparative advantage in terms of labour costs (labour hours used per unit of output produced) is the basis for specialisation in the respective commodity. Specialisations by individual countries in different commodities lead to mutually gainful trade across nations. The Ricardian theory of comparative advantage thus states that countries export goods in which they have comparative labour productivity advantage. Trade takes place as comparative labour productivities differ between countries irrespective of their absolute labour productivity advantages.

According to the H-O theory, a country's comparative advantage is determined by its relative factor scarcity (i.e., its factor endowment ratios, relative to the rest of the world or a set of countries) and cost differences resulting from differences in factor prices across countries. The H-O theory proposes that a country's comparative advantage lies in the goods that make use of the factor in which it has relative abundance. Succinctly stated, the H-O theory predicts that a country exports the product(s) that use its relatively abundant factor(s) intensively and imports the product(s) using its relatively scarce factor(s) intensively. A country is relatively labour abundant if it has a higher ratio of labour to other factors than does the rest of the world and a product is relatively labour intensive if labour costs are a greater share of its value than they are of the value of other products. A significant implication of the H-O theory is that the exchange of commodities internationally is thus indirect factor arbitrage that can under some circumstances lead to complete elimination of factor price differentials. The H-O theory in the original is with reference to two countries that are engaged in free trade with each producing the same pair of commodities in a purely competitive setting, supported by constant returns to scale technology that is shared by both countries. Each commodity is produced separately with inputs of two factors of production that, in each country, are supplied perfectly inelastically. The predictive power of the theory is weakened when factor intensity reversals are admitted so that an unequivocal classification of goods by factor intensity becomes impossible: commodities which are relatively capital intensive under a particular set of factor prices may be relatively labour intensive under another.

Theoretical advancement beyond the traditional explanations for trade based on comparative advantage is said to have begun after Second World War (WWII) and especially after the trade agreements of 1950s and 1960s when trade in similar commodities among nations became prominent (Krugman, 2008). Trade in the post WWII period was in the nature of intra-industry trade. As explained by Krugman, Balassa (1966) had earlier made clear the basis of similar-similar trade with continuing relevance of the theory of comparative advantage, when he stated that each country produced only a part of the range of potential products within each industry, importing those goods it did not produce, as 'specialisation in a narrower range of machinery and intermediate products will permit the exploitation of economies of scale though the lengthening of production runs'. The concept of IRS (increasing returns to scale) is thus introduced in the new theory along with other market imperfections.

The old trade theory is focused on trade being created on account of differences between nations. Instead, Krugman laid emphasis on the geographical concentration of varieties using the IRS as an explanation. Given resource constraints and imperfect competition each country cannot produce all goods but would produce some unique varieties and buy some of every variety thus creating the base for two way trade between similar or even identical nations. The Helpman-Krugman synthesis model explains both intra- and inter-industry trade. Allowing for relative factor abundance differences between the nations and in a two sector model—labour intensive and capital intensive, netting out the IIT (intra-industry trade), the trade pattern is explained to follow the H-O theorem, that is labour abundant nations will export relatively more labour intensive goods. Further, if IIT is added trade between similar countries is also explained. Thus, the new trade theory that includes imperfect competition and increasing returns to scale helped understand many real world aspects that could not be explained by the old theory.

Additionally, new trade models introduce the elements of strategic behaviour, new growth theory and political economy arguments. Models based on market imperfections and strategic behaviour provide justification for state intervention.

Inclusion of imperfections—imperfect competition, increasing returns to scale, differentiated products—that led to the evolution of new trade theory has in turn led to the notion of strategic trade theory as proposed and formulated by Brander and Spencer in 1985 wherein situations of imperfect markets, internal economies of scale allow for aggressive strategic trade policies like subsidies, reciprocal dumping, etc. The main objective of strategic trade policy is that it includes support and stimulus to the growth of sectors regarded as strategic aiming to increase national income. Strategic trade theory shows that in certain circumstances a government can take action such that it may increase the country's share of rents captured by traders.

So, new trade theory and international trade research has since the 1980s been much focused upon the implications of relaxation of the assumption of perfect markets and to account for the effects of imperfect competition, increasing returns to scale and strategic behaviour. Both the old and new trade theories are however criticised for having failed to recognise the implications for trade of differential economic development of nations. More recently, however, there has been the rise of applied research that is focused on testing such theories as also on analysing policy developments evident in the economic integration processes across different regions of the world. Trade policy weaves together a variety of instruments and possible outcomes as it is invariably situated in a sectoral context and specific economic conditions in which it is to operate and involves interactions with other polices. Trade policies based on a complex interplay of domestic and international factors need to resolve trade-offs between the various interested and affected parties.

In a further progression therefore the 'new-new' trade theory and its implied 'new-new' trade policy states that it is the 'firms' perspective that is primary in trade as against that of the country or industry. The firms that trade have to undertake higher costs to establish and sustain themselves in international markets as 'information asymmetries' may lead to uncertainty and higher risks regarding exchange rate valuation and regulatory changes in the foreign markets. Typically therefore only the most productive firms trade. Instruments of trade policy negotiation and evaluation of trade agreements following the principle of 'reciprocity' must be designed in the light of this understanding and therefore negotiated not just for benefits to existing trading firms but also to those that diversify to take advantage of new markets. Technically this implies that the focus of negotiations should be on extensive margins as against solely on intensive margins and the objective should be to resolve uncertainty in the minds of potential exporters regarding international markets. And, to the extent that market entry costs if high, on account of uncertainty and consequent failure, would deter firms from trading, the policy emphasis ought to be on reducing the fixed costs. Often when tariffs are low, fixed costs are reflected in the form of cumbersome and protracted entry barriers and procedures to get goods across borders. Trade facilitation in the context would assume added importance (Ciuriak *et al.*, 2011). Among the many uncertainties therefore to be reduced in this context would be those faced by exporters on account of NTBs and issues related to trade facilitation. This is particularly relevant in regions or between countries that are or aim at becoming part of a supply chain. Facilitating easy passage across borders would be paramount in such cases. Policy action in this context would therefore emphasise on simplifying cross border customs procedures and installation of compatible standards and regulation. This aspect gains further in importance in the post global financial crisis scenario when south-south trade cooperation is imperative for generating export demand for developing countries and trade is increasingly being led by supply chain linkages.

Quantitative analysis of trade policy has gained importance in the context of rapid economic and trade liberalisation undertaken by developing economies. With trade contributing an increasing proportion of total GDP (gross domestic product) in India, the analysis gains relevance. A careful examination of trade policy instruments, negotiating strategies and potential impact would help shape and evaluate government policy in the context of India's global and regional economic integration. Policymakers need to have access to an assessment of potential economic gains like the scope for trade creation and diversion that is based on careful data analysis as also drawing from analysis of past and other country relevant experiences.

Applied international trade research is different from trade theory propositions, in particular in the policy arena. It requires a broad set of tools that can be quite different from those emphasised in pure academia. Familiarity with concepts including gravity models, trade data nomenclature etc., would be called for in the application of trade theory to real world policy environment analysis. Trade policy analysis invariably includes formulation of models where the structure may be drawn according to the context and available data so as to provide sensible results. Accurate and latest/current data are of singular importance in such exercises.

1.2 India: Economic Reforms and Growth

A shift in India's trade policy with a conscious attempt to integrate with the global economy was observed during the 1990s. Policy measures towards trade liberalisation, although, initiated in the late 1970s and subsequently observed in the 1980s were piecemeal and incremental in nature. These changes that included export oriented and directed schemes have been categorised as easing out restrictions for business and are therefore termed as pro-business changes rather than indicative of any major signalling towards a pro-market economy. The policy changes during this period were influenced, among others, by recommendations of two prominent committees set up during this period: The Committee on Export-Import Policies and Procedures[3] and Report of the Committee on Trade Policies.[4] Following the recommendations of the Alexander Committee, selective import liberalisation measures primarily for some capital goods and raw materials were initiated along with some special measures to boost export of project goods. The Abid Hussain Committee recommended a greater harmonisation of the export policies and growth process as also the formulation of trade policy with a longer time perspective. This was implemented with the Export-Import policy being announced for a longer period of 1985-1988.[5]

The systemic reforms undertaken against a background of the BoP (balance of payment) crisis in 1991 combined the task of India's integration with the world economy with that of fiscal consolidation. The former was undertaken through a series of policy initiatives including dismantling barriers to foreign trade and investment and the latter through a rationalisation of the direct and indirect tax structure. Measures like removal of QRs (quantitative restrictions), lowering of tariff barriers and introduction of a market determined exchange rate were initiated with regard to trade liberalisation.[6] Capital flows were simultaneously facilitated into the economy as financial markets were opened to FIIs (foreign institutional investors) and more and more industrial sectors to FDI (foreign direct investment). The industrial sector was also witness to other reforms like de-licensing, privatisation, de-reservation and the institutional reform like the setting up of the Competition Commission of India.

3. Chairman: P.C. Alexander, 1978.
4. Chairman: Abid Hussain, 1984.
5. Beginning 1992-1997, Export-Import policies in India are now announced for a period of five years.
6. During the early 1990s, India's unilateral trade liberalisation was restricted to the manufacturing sector. During the years 1995 to 2001, the remaining restrictions (QRs) on imports were gradually removed in a large measure in response to international pressures. The first of these pressures came from Uruguay Round negotiations on textiles and clothing (Agreement on Textiles and Clothing, phasing out of the Multi Fibre Arrangement [MFA]), the second from a dispute brought against India at the WTO in the matter of imposing QRs on imports under the BoPs clause of the GATT (Article XVIII (B)). See, Goldar, 2005.

While the reform process in 1991 was an outcome of the compelling circumstances that developed in India owing to the BoP crisis and the SAP (structural adjustment programme) as part of the bailout loan from the International Monetary Fund (IMF), it may also be recognised that India averted default thereby allowing itself an element of independence to choose the pace and sequence of reforms. Many of the reviews undertaken in the wake of the Washington Consensus's[7] inability to trigger growth in Latin American and the transition economies have invariably cited India as a unique case that has succeeded because of its ability to mix traditional thinking and growth strategy with a liberalisation strategy. In the Indian case, effort was also made to go beyond the prescribed policy measures and pick the most appropriate (conducive to domestic conditions) lessons from countries that had earlier experienced economic growth by following export-oriented growth models—especially East Asia. This is evident from the change in the orientation of India's foreign policy wherein a conscious aligning with the erstwhile miracle economies to draw lessons of liberalisation was undertaken. India's 'look east policy' (LEP) initiated in 1991 was a conscious attempt towards establishing a close economic alliance with successful economies of East Asia and Association of Southeast Asian Nations (ASEAN). The LEP acquired the dimension of regionalism in the next decade with India's first FTAs being announced/signed with the ASEAN and member countries of Thailand and Singapore. This aspect is discussed later in the monograph.

The outcome of the move towards economic liberalisation that began in 1991 has been a relatively higher growth trajectory for India in comparison with the decades preceding the reforms. India registered an average rate of growth of GDP of 6.6 per cent in the period 1991-2010 as against the much lower, below 4.0 per cent, rate of growth that it experienced in the three decades between 1950 and 1980, and the modest acceleration thereafter to 5.4 per

7. Coined in 1989, the term was used by John Williamson to describe a set of 10 policy reform measures that were required in Latin America. The term over time has come to be associated with reforms under the SAP of the IMF for countries that borrow to avert/overcome a financial crisis. See, Williamson, 2004.

cent in the 1980s.[8] While growth rate has fluctuated over the two decades post economic reforms, in the years 2003-2008 India registered an average rate of growth of 8.7 per cent accompanied by macroeconomic stability as reflected in the average inflation rate that was comfortably around 5.0 per cent, combined (centre and state) fiscal deficit that was 6.1 per cent of GDP (4.1% in 2007-08) and a current account deficit maintained at less than 1.0 per cent. The Indian economy was also one of the first to register recovery to its pre-crisis growth rates in the aftermath of the global financial crisis and registered a 9.3 per cent rate of growth in 2010. India has also simultaneously integrated itself with the global economy and its international trade volumes have been growing faster than GDP. In 2011, exports grew at a rate of 33.8 per cent that was among the highest in the world and higher than the rate of export growth of 20.3 per cent registered by the Chinese economy. Rising significance of exports for the Indian economy is evident in the growing proportion of exports as a share of GDP. Exports of goods and services, as a percentage of GDP have increased from 14 per cent in 2000-01 to 22 per cent in 2010-11 and 24 per cent in 2012.

As progress at the World Trade Organization (WTO) slowed down in the 2000s and the Doha Development Agenda (DDA) saw little forward movement[9] India entered into several preferential

8. The higher average growth experienced in the 1980s was not stable as the piecemeal, incremental and capacity easing strategy had taken the economy on an unviable growth path. This was reflected in the increased growth in this period being accompanied by a spiralling government deficit that spilled over to a burgeoning level of ECBs (external commercial borrowings) that in turn could not be supported by rising level of exports because the underlying and necessary export competitiveness had not been achieved. Growth in the 1980s was thus fragile

9. At the multilateral level, India signed the Marrakesh agreement (1994) that led to the establishment of the WTO with sector specific commitments towards liberalising trade regimes. Post Marrakesh, India was opposed to the expansionary design of the developed world to include non-trade issues like Investment, Competition Policy, Transparency in Government Procurement and Trade Facilitation (Singapore Issues) and core labour standards in the negotiations as also to the initiation of a new round given the difficulties of implementation of the Uruguay round agreements. India signed the Doha Agreement (2001) for a new round only after being granted concessions on implementation issues, flexibilities regarding the TRIPS agreement and exclusion of Singapore issues. With its increasing integration with the global economy India has now acquired the stance of a pro-active player at the WTO negotiations. The Doha round has however been slow to progress given the differential negotiating stance of the developed and developing countries on issues of non-agricultural market access, agricultural subsidies and services sector liberalisation.

trading and economic cooperation arrangements predominantly with countries in East Asia, South and South East Asia. PTAs allow for the economy to be exposed to competitive forces through preferential access to domestic markets, creation of trade and market diversification. This trend is assisted by as also should reinforce the reforms induced competitive market environment that has given the Indian industry the necessary push to improve quality and achieve cost efficiency. Economic liberalisation, it is considered, has made a positive impact by creating a policy environment that has provided entrepreneurs with the flexibility they need to make their own decisions on technology, location, size of investment etc., all of which have a bearing on productivity and competitive strength. Notwithstanding the positive outcomes of liberalisation, concerns regarding the size of current account deficit in India remain and the approach paper to the XIIth Plan has emphasised the need for a fundamental change in Indian manufacturing and trade pattern of importing finished goods and exporting raw material.

1.2.1 India and China: The Comparative Context

Interest in comparative analysis of the Indian and Chinese economies has been generated owing to the rapid pace of economic growth that the two economies have experienced after undertaking significant and systemic economic reforms. Together the two economies, India with its unprecedented growth averaging over 8 per cent in the period 2003-2008 and China with its consistent growth performance of double digit growth rates in the 2000s, have contributed to the shift in the centre of gravity of the global economy from the West to the East. Since the onset of the global financial crisis of 2008-09, India and China were among the first few economies to have recovered to their pre-crisis levels of growth in 2010. A natural outcome of the economic dynamism reflected in their growth processes has been their increased contribution to the global growth process with India contributing about 3 per cent and China about 12 per cent of global output.

For both India and China, recovery from the global financial crisis of 2008-09 has been easier and quicker than the rest of the world. In

2010, China with a rate of economic growth of 10.3 per cent made a return to its pre-crisis double digit pace of growth. India also recorded its pre-crisis growth of over 8.0 per cent in the same year. Relative to the rest of the region and global growth trends the two economies stand out in their performance and are therefore being seen as the saviours of the global economy in the course of recovery from the global financial crisis. However, the global expectations are far greater with regard to the Chinese economy than the Indian economy as the former has on a sustained basis contributed a larger proportion of the global output. China contributed almost 13 per cent of the global output in 2009 having increased from about 4 per cent in 1990-91. The Chinese contribution comprises about a third of the developing South's and almost half of developing Asia's contribution to the world output. In the period when record expansion was registered in world growth, that is, over the years 2004 to 2007, China shared global growth leadership with the United States while in the current slowdown it is perceived as the undisputed chief driver of world growth (Bergsten *et al.*, 2008). In contrast India's contribution to the global output is modest having increased from 3 per cent in 1990-91 to a little over 5 per cent in 2009.

The story of outward orientation as reflected in the global trade integration of the two economies is also spectacular. China initiated its reform process in 1978 with policies to attract FDI so as to promote exports. Trade promotion and easing out of the strict and complex import control regime gained ground in 1992 when China was in a preparatory mode for its accession to the WTO in 2001. India undertook systemic economic reforms and liberalisation of its trade policies in 1991. Prior attempts in 1979 and 1984-85, as discussed earlier, were tentative and marginal with incremental and/ or unsustainable growth outcomes.

The economic reforms have led to a removal of most border NTBs and internal licensing restrictions in India. Nominal applied tariffs came down from an average of 100 per cent in 1985 to 13 per cent by 2008-09. The maximum tariff on non-agricultural goods, save for a few items, has come down to 10 per cent. In agriculture, though, tariffs and NTBs remain much higher. The average applied tariff in agriculture is 32 per cent. The maximum MFN tariff is 246 per cent. India has bound 74 per cent of its tariffs in the WTO at an average rate of 50 per cent. The gap between India's protection level and that of other developing countries has narrowed and is much closer to that of the ASEAN and Chinese levels. The trade weighted average tariff rate on all goods in India is at 6.0 per cent in comparison with 4.1 per cent for Indonesia and 4.3 per cent for China. Overall, though, India continues to be more protectionist than the East Asian economies. Simple average applied tariff is 10.1 and 32.0 per cent for manufactured and agricultural goods respectively in India. In comparison, the simple average applied tariff rate in manufacturing and agriculture is 6.6 and 8.4 in Indonesia and 8.7 and 15.6 in China.

Trade now constitutes an important component of economic activity of both countries with its share in GDP for China far outpacing that for India. At the time of initiation of its economic reforms in 1978, China's openness index[10] was at a low of 6.6 per cent and close to that for India at 6.4 per cent. In 1991, when India initiated its trade liberalisation programme, China had already started to reap the gains of economic reforms as reflected in an almost three times increase in the value of its openness index since 1978. India's openness index rose after the economic reforms started to make an impact in the late 1990s. The openness index increased to 22.9 per cent in 2010, also a three times increase from the pre-reform period but well below that of the Chinese openness index of almost 32.0 per cent in the same year. The differential rates of trade expansion for the two economies are particularly apparent with regard to the volume of exports. In 2008, China exported a total of 1.6 trillion goods and services that comprised 8.0 per cent of world exports against India's $263 billion or 1.3 per cent of world exports (Wignraja, 2011). China's larger presence in the global trade scenario, owing to a prior start on the economic reforms front, is therefore evident. India, while having made significant strides from its pre-liberalisation days, is a relatively smaller player in terms of global

10. Openness index is defined as the ratio of export plus imports of goods and services to GDP.

trade volumes. Overall, India accounts for 2.4 per cent of world trade, well behind China's 10.7 per cent.

The analysis of the structure and pattern of the comparative advantage is relevant in this context as it provides evidence of economic dynamism. The comparative analysis with China and in the regional context helps shed light on the evolving competition as India integrates with the global and regional economies. Comparative analysis based on rigorous empirical exercises of trade and specialisation patterns is helpful in drawing appropriate conclusions in this respect. The following chapter presents the evidence for the structure of India's RCA drawing on comparisons with the Chinese comparative advantage structure where relevant and significant.

2

Revealed Comparative Advantage

A country's trade pattern should be ideally accounted for by direct measurement of factor and technology endowments. However as endowment data are rarely available, RCA (revealed comparative advantage) indices based on trade data are used. As such, therefore, they cannot be used to compare actual with potential sectoral trade patterns. It is also well known that measuring comparative advantage and testing the Hecksher-Ohlin (H-O) theory have some difficulties since relative prices under autarky are not observable. Given these facts, Balassa (1965) proposes that comparative advantage is "revealed" by observed trade patterns, and in line with the theory, one needs pre-trade relative prices which are not observable. Thus, inferring comparative advantage from observed data is named "revealed" comparative advantage. In practice, this is a commonly accepted method of analysing trade data. Balassa (1965) formulated the index that tries to identify whether a country has a RCA rather than to determine the underlying sources of comparative advantage.[1]

We discuss below the concept of RCA as formulated by Balassa (1965) and most commonly used for empirical analysis along with alternative formulations that have since been developed owing to the possible 'noise' in the original Balassa formula. The post global financial crisis reconsideration of the global bilateral trade, imbalances and significance of networked production therein that has led to a re-evaluation of RCA on the basis of domestic value addition is also discussed. In addition, data induced limitations

1. Harrigan, 1997; Beck, 2003; Romalis, 2004; Yeaple and Golub, 2007; Nunn, 2007; Manova, 2008; Morrow, 2010, Chor, 2010 constitute the large empirical literature investigating the role of various sources of comparative advantage

to the application of the concept of RCA to services trade are also highlighted.

The concept of RCA as proposed by Balassa (1965; 1977; 1979; 1986) analysed the RCA measure in manufacturing and across industries. The concept pertains to the relative trade performance of individual countries in particular commodities. On the assumption that the commodity pattern of trade reflects the inter-country differences in relative costs as well as in non-price factors, this is assumed to 'reveal' the comparative advantage of the trading countries. The factors that contribute to movements in RCA are economic and include structural change, improved world demand and trade specialisation.

Balassa's (1965) measure of relative export performance by country and industry/commodity is defined as a country's share of world exports of a commodity divided by its share of world exports. The index for country i commodity j is calculated as follows:

$RCA_{ij} = (X_{ij}/X_{wj})/(X_i/X_w)$.

where:

X_{ij} = i^{th} country's exports of commodity j.

X_{wj} = World exports of commodity j.

X_i = Total exports of country i.

X_w = Total world exports.

The index has a relatively simple interpretation. If it takes a value of greater than unity the country has a RCA in that product. Ballance *et al.* (1987) suggested that the RCA index can be interpreted in three ways. Firstly, each index provides a demarcation between countries, that reveal a comparative advantage in a particular sector and those countries that do not. Secondly, it quantifies the sector specific degree of comparative advantage enjoyed by one country or set of countries. Thirdly, it allows for possible cross-country and cross sector rankings according to their specific values. This has however been criticised and it is said that the Balassa's RCA index is not a reflection of comparative advantage for each country, across sectors

(Yeats, 1985).[2] Hinloopen and Marrewijk (2001) further state that it is not clear *a priori* if a specific value of Balassa index implies the same extent of comparative advantage for different countries. This aspect has been discussed by Hinloopen and Marrewijk with a reference sample of EU-12 countries' exports to a single country Japan, correcting in the process, any biases that may arise due to differential market access, distance, heterogeneous tastes in case of exports to a global market. The 'clean' comparative advantage distribution so derived differs considerably across countries thus making cross-country comparisons difficult. De Benedictis and Tamberi (2004), also present the superiority of the ordinal analysis, both in time and space of the index values and the many interesting insights of comparative advantage that it can provide while a cardinal interpretation of the Balassa index values, according to them, should be considered informative for cross-country and inter-temporal comparisons only after controlling for possible misinterpretations. Also, it needs to be accepted by both applied economists and policymakers that in reality the RCA indices need not be truly representative of the underlying real comparative advantage as it can be altered by government policy like export subsidy, import restrictions and or other protectionist policies.

The advantage of using the Balassa comparative advantage index is that it considers the intrinsic advantage of a particular export commodity and is consistent with changes in an economy's relative factor endowment and productivity. The disadvantage, however, is that it cannot distinguish improvements in factor endowments and pursuit of appropriate trade policies by a country. The RCA index does not discriminate between comparative advantage that is 'inherent' in an economy and that which is 'policy-induced'. So that in any analysis, the scope for policy induced distortions in the RCA should be recognised. Another disadvantage of the RCA index is that it is

2. Yeats calculated the correlation between RCA ranks across sectors and across 47 countries based on 1976-78 trade data which was aggregated over the three years and found significant (at 5% level) correlation coefficient for only 60 per cent of the cases. Later studies have however not necessarily corroborated this finding. Laursen (1998) for example, in a set of 19 OECD countries, 22 sectors over 24 years finds only 2 per cent insignificant rank correlations at 1 per cent level of significance and none at 5 per cent level.

asymmetric, i.e., unbounded for those sectors with a RCA, but it has a zero lower bound for those sectors with a comparative disadvantage. Alternative measures of comparative advantage have been proposed, some that refer to imports rather than exports applying the same formula as above, but where X is replaced by M. Another solution is proposed by Laursen (1998) in which case the measure is obtained as (RCA-1)/(RCA+1) and is called the Revealed Symmetric Comparative Advantage (RSCA). The RSCA has a range of -1 to +1.

Alternative definitions of RCA have also been proposed by Vollrath (1987; 1989) and Vollrath and Vo (1990): relative trade advantage that accounts for exports as well as imports. It is calculated as the difference between relative export advantage and the relative import advantage (RCA1). Vollrath's relative export advantage is different from the Balassa index as it eliminates country and commodity double counting and accounts for all traded goods and all countries, thus being a global index. The logarithm of the export advantage is the second alternative (RCA2) given by Vollrath and the third (RCA3), called the revealed competitiveness, is the difference of the logarithm of the export advantage and logarithm of the import advantage. The distinction of Vollrath's indices of revealed competitive advantage thus calculated is that they eliminate country and commodity double counting in world trade.

$RCA1^i_a = RXA^i_a - RMA^i_a$

Where:

$RXA^i_a = (X^i_a / X^i_n)/(X^r_a / X^r_n)$ and $RMA^i_a = (M^i_a / M^i_n)/(M^r_a / M^r_n)$

$RCA2^i_a = Ln(RXA^i_a)$

$RCA3^i_a = Ln(RXA^i_a) - Ln(RMA^i_a)$

RXA and RMA identify relative export advantage and relative import advantage, respectively; and superscript r refers to the world minus country i while subscript n refers to all traded commodities minus commodity.

Vollrath (1991)[3] undertakes a survey comparing the theoretical underpinnings of the different measures of the RCA. Highlighting the gaps and constraints of quantifying and empirically measuring comparative advantage, he states that the most basic limitation arises from the fact that the theoretical concept of comparative advantage is specified in terms of pre-trade relative prices in a distortion-less world where markets work perfectly while researchers in the real world are only able to use data generated from trade flows post trade equilibria.

The theoretical foundations of the Balassa index have been criticised for not truly reflecting the original Ricardian concept of comparative advantage (Bowen, 1983; Vollrath, 1991). Hinloopen and Marrewijk, 2001 state that despite detailed theoretical discussions on the Balassa index (as in Kunimoto, 1977; Hillman, 1980; Bowen, 1983; 1985; 1986; Ballance *et al.*, 1985; 1986; 1987; Vollrath, 1991; and Bowen *et al.*, 1998) distribution of the Balassa index cannot be derived theoretically. Attempts to derive theoretically consistent quantitative measures of comparative advantage, as an alternative to the Balassa (1965) index of RCA, have been more recently made by Costinot *et al.* (2012) and Leromaine and Orifice (2013). Costinot *et al.* provide a theoretical basis to estimate the impact of observed productivity differences on pattern of trade across countries and industries so as to explore the quantitative implications of Ricardo's ideas, not relying in the process, as they state on ad hoc measures of export performance such as total exports to the rest of the world, total exports to third markets, or bilateral net exports. Constrained by the availability of trade flows and productivity data, the quantitative estimation is undertaken for the year 1997 with a limited data set of 21 countries that includes 18 European countries and Japan, Korea and the US. The elasticity with which increases in observed productivity levels, ceteris paribus, lead to increased exports is

3. Identifies 10 alternative indices of RCA and establishes the evolutionary linkages. The Balassa index and the three indices of RCA are found to be the most satisfying in terms of links with their theoretical underpinnings. RCA2 is the preferred index relative to the other indices as exports are considered to be impacted more by relative efficiencies and relative factor endowments rather than policy instruments as is true of imports.

estimated at a positive value in agreement with Ricardian theory and robust to alternative estimation procedures. Leromaine and Orifice use the Costinot *et al.* idea with an extended sample, greater product disaggregation (HS-2 and HS-4) within the manufacturing sector (excluding sectors HS-27: minerals and mineral fuels and HS-97: art and artworks), and a longer time period to develop a new measure of RCA that is based solely on productivity differentials. Econometric and computational complexity in terms of managing the number of fixed effects with increasing product disaggregation is a clear limitation of this measure.

So while innovations to make the RCA index more theoretically consistent and true to the Ricardian model continue, scope for practical applications of these alternatives is yet limited. The Balassa index therefore continues to be used extensively[4] for simplicity of formula, calculations, data availability and interpretation of patterns of specialisation underlying trade flows.

2.1 Empirical Evidence

Batra and Khan (2005) make the first systematic attempt to examine the structure of comparative advantage enjoyed by India individually and in a comparative framework with China, in the global market using the Balassa (1965) index and export data. As RCA at the aggregate level may differ from that at the dis-aggregated level, the analysis is undertaken at the sector (2-digit) and commodity level (6-digit) of the harmonised system (HS) of trade classification. The RCA analysis at the sector-level has been undertaken for all 97 sectors of the HS classification for both India and China for the year 2003. A reference analysis is undertaken for 2000 as the year immediately preceding China's accession to the WTO in 2001. The comparative advantage structure has also been analysed in terms of its factor intensity at the 2 and 3 digit level of SITC (Rev. 3)

4. Ariovich (1979); Reza (1983); Amiti (1999); Ferto and Hubbard (2003); Richardson and Zhang (1999); Amighini *et al.* (2011).

classification. Inter-temporal variations over the period 2000-2003 are also discussed for both countries.[5]

The analysis shows that in 2003 out of a total of 4,664 commodities of India's exports to the world, it enjoys comparative advantage in 1,512 commodities. Sector-wise, India shows comparative advantage in 42 of the 97 sectors for which analysis is undertaken and the sector with maximum RCA index value of 17.4 is HS-50 (silk). This is closely followed by HS-13 (lac, gums, vegetable saps and extracts nes), HS-71 (pearls, precious stones, metals, coins), HS-57 (carpets and other textile floor coverings), HS-52 (cotton), HS-63 (other made textile articles, sets, worn clothing etc).[6] At the disaggregated commodity level, maximum number of commodities with comparative advantage is found to be concentrated in HS-29 (organic chemicals), which contributes 8 per cent of the total commodity-wise comparative advantage that India enjoys in the world market. This is followed by HS-52 (cotton), HS-72 (iron and steel), HS-61 (articles of apparel accessories, not knit crochet etc.), each having a 5 per cent share.

The pattern of comparative advantage varies at different levels of aggregation. Sector HS-84 (nuclear reactors, boilers, machinery etc.) contributes 5 per cent of the total commodity-wise comparative advantage that India holds in the world market while being disadvantageously placed at the aggregate level. The only sector that is placed among the top 10 sectors based on the criteria of comparative advantage at the aggregate level as well as on the basis of number of constituent commodities with comparative advantage is HS-52 (cotton). Sectors like organic chemicals, cotton and iron and steel retain their top position when ranked according to comparative advantage at the aggregate and disaggregate level.

5. Notwithstanding the short period of three years, inter-temporal analysis is undertaken by the authors to gauge the extent of dynamism in China's comparative advantage structure after accession to the WTO in 2001. Hence, the reference period starts with the year immediately preceding accession and ends with the latest year for which data is available at the time of the study. Evidence of some changes in the RCA structure at the commodity level is evident. The SRCC (Spearman Rank Correlation Coefficient) methodology, discussed later in this section is a useful technique for comparative analysis and may be used for future research on the subject.

6. Detailed tables for all aspects discussed in this section are available in Batra and Khan (2005).

In comparison with India, China enjoys comparative advantage in 1,828 of its 4,923 commodity exports to the world market. Sector-wise China holds comparative advantage in 47 sectors. Sectors like HS-46 (manufactures of plaiting material) and HS-67 (bird skin, feathers, artificial flowers, human hair) rank at the top according to the RCA index value. At the dis-aggregated level China's comparative advantage is highest in the electrical and electronic equipment sector which with 129 commodities contributes 8 per cent of the total commodity wise comparative advantage that China enjoys in the world market. This is closely followed by sectors like organic chemicals, articles of apparel, not knit/crocheted. Other sectors with significant number of commodities which enjoy comparative advantage are organic chemicals, inorganic chemicals and articles of apparel knit/crocheted or not knit/crocheted. Like HS-52 (cotton) in India, the sector that is advantageously placed both at the aggregate and dis-aggregated level for China is HS-63 (other made textiles, sets, worn clothing).

As regards inter-temporal variation in sector-wise comparative advantage the analysis reveals that for India even while the number of sectors with comparative advantage in the world market and the top 10 among these are the same between 2000 and 2003, the composition has changed. Among the sectors that have lost advantage HS-30 (pharmaceutical products) figures prominently while HS-28 (inorganic chemicals) finds a place among sectors that have gained advantage. Sectors like works of art, collectors pieces, antiques and ores, slag and ash make an entry among India's most competitive sectors in 2003. The sectors with maximum number of commodities with comparative advantage are also same across the two years. The only sector that gains comparative advantage in 2003 is HS-72 (iron and steel). As in India's case, China shows little change in the number of sectors that are comparatively advantageously placed in the global market. Of the 10 most competitive sectors 8 are common to both the years 2000 and 2003.

Dynamic changes in the structure of comparative advantage are also analysed using the Spearman Rank Correlation (SRC) coefficient.[7] The analysis is undertaken for manufacturing as a whole as also for individual sectors within manufacturing. For manufacturing as a whole the SRC coefficient for both India and China as expected over the short period of 2000-2003 is high (0.8 and 0.9 respectively) and indicates no major changes in their structure of comparative advantage. For India, change is however evident within manufacturing for sectors like HS-81 (other base metals, cermets, articles thereof); HS-89 ships, boats and other floating structures and HS-31 (fertilisers) for which the SRC is observed to be the lowest. For sector HS-41 (raw hides and skin [other than fur skins] and leather), the value of the SRC coefficient is negative indicating RCA reversals within the sector. This is clear from further analysis that shows 50 per cent of the commodities in this sector having experienced a reversal from being disadvantageously placed to having gained comparative advantage in the world market over the period 2000 to 2003. Overall, high, modest, and low structural change is evident in almost an equal number of sectors in the pattern of RCA for India in these three years.

In a comparative analysis of India and China, it is observed that there are 26 sectors where both the countries enjoy comparative advantage in the global market. India's comparative advantage is in the agriculture and allied sectors and this gets further consolidated in 2003. The other categories where India consolidates its advantage vis-à-vis China is in the resource-based manufactures and miscellaneous manufactures. China is relatively advantageously placed in the world market in both resource-based manufactures and machines and equipment category with the former comprising a larger number of sectors with advantage. In resource-based manufactures, China gained comparative advantage in sectors like glass and glassware, tin and articles thereof while in category of machine and equipment the advantage gained in 2003 lay in nuclear reactors, boilers machinery. India reveals no sector-wise advantage in the machinery and equipment category. The advantage held by China in organic

7. The SRC coefficient is a non-parametric test often used to test for independence between two variables. The range of possible values is from -1 to+1. A value close to the extremes is indicative of perfect correlation, positive or negative. A value of zero indicates no correlation.

chemicals in 2000 is lost in 2003, while India continues to enjoy comparative advantage in organic chemicals in both the years.

2.1.1 RCA by Factor Intensity

Batra and Khan (2005) also analyse the RCA in terms of factor intensity for the manufacturing sector that contributes 95 and 88 per cent of the total exports for China and India respectively in 2003. The factor intensity analysis has been undertaken using the SITC (Rev. 3) classification. The SITC has been developed by the United Nations (UN) with the intention of classifying traded products not only on the basis of their material and physical properties, but also according to the stage of processing, and their economic functions in order to facilitate economic analysis. The HS classification while having the advantage of detail and dis-aggregation is restricted only to a precise breakdown of the products' individual categories. For analysing comparative advantage by factor intensity, therefore, SITC is a preferred classification.

The exports classified at the HS-6 digit level of classification are as a first step mapped on to the SITC classification at the 5-digit level using the UNCOMTRADE classification registry and then aggregated to three and 2-digit level to facilitate product classification by factor intensity. The analysis of comparative advantage in terms of factor intensity is based on the UNCTAD classification at the 2-digit and the ETA (empirical trade analysis) and WDI (Williamson Davidson Institute) classification systems at the 3-digit level.[8]

Of the 1,512 commodities where India enjoys comparative advantage in the world market, 1,272 commodities are classified as manufactures at the 5-digit level of the SITC classification. At the 2-digit level, a predominant share comprising 573 commodities

---

8. The authors report that the factor intensity analysis at the 2-digit level of classification has been undertaken using the UNCTAD, OECD and Anderson and Garnaut (1980) system of classifications. At the 3-digit level, the ETA, WDI and world matrix of sectoral economic data (hwwa) classification systems have been used. The discussion in the study is however based largely on the UNCTAD at the 2-digit level and ETA and WDI at the 3-digit level of classification respectively as these are the most comprehensive systems of classification. The UNCTAD system of classification is based on details relating to human capital, technology, and capital intensity of the manufactured commodities.

in 2003 are resource and labour intensive as per the UNCTAD classification. Of the remaining manufactures, 301 commodities are such that they make a high demand for skill, technology, capital and scale while 191 and 134 commodities make a low and medium demand for these factors respectively. The resource and labour intensive category of manufactures is dominated by sectors like HS-65 (textiles, yarn, fabric, made-up articles n.e.s. and related products) and HS-61 and HS-62 (articles of apparel and clothing accessories). Commodities from the organic chemicals followed by inorganic chemicals sectors are conspicuous in the category with high demand for skill, technology, capital, and scale. The picture is observed to be similar in 2000 with the resource and labour intensive category being the predominant items of manufactures where India holds comparative advantage in the world market. At the 3-digit level of classification also labour intensive and resource intensive are the largest two categories of international specialisation for Indian exports in both the reference years.

In case of the Chinese economy of the total 1,828 commodities where it enjoys comparative advantage in the world market 1,631 are classified as manufactured items in the SITC classification. A majority of these manufactured items (794) fall in the resource and labour intensive categories as per the UNCTAD classification. This is followed by the set of commodities that demand high (402), low (196) and medium (172) skill, technology, capital, and scale. In the resource and labour intensive categories, maximum number of commodities are drawn from the sectors HS-65 (textiles, yarn, fabric, made-up articles n.e.s and related products) and articles of apparel and clothing accessories. Organic chemicals followed by inorganic chemicals dominate the high demand for skill, capital, technology, and scale category. Again, as in India's case no major change is observed from the structure of comparative advantage for China in 2000. At the 3-digit level, the conclusions are reinforced as the majority of commodities with comparative advantage belong to the resource and labour intensive categories.

For both India and China, science-based industries contribute less than 10 per cent of the comparative advantage that the two countries hold in the manufacturing sector in the global market. In absolute numbers, though, China's number of science-based industries with advantage is double that of India and although the two countries enjoy advantage in the same industries, China outscores India in almost all of these. India's comparative advantage is marginally higher than China's in the medicinal and pharmaceutical products, which incidentally is also the predominant sector for India. For China, the product category of photographic apparatus, equipment and, optical goods dominates.

Veeramani (2008) has presented, for India and China, the percentage of commodities with RCA more than one in five different factor intensity categories. The RCA has been computed for commodities at the SITC-3-digit level using average export value over each five year sub-period within the overall reference period that extends from 1980-1984 to 2000-2003. The analysis shows that there has been a gradual gain in comparative advantage for both India and China in human capital and technology intensive commodities. Relative to India, China holds comparative advantage for a larger number of commodities in unskilled labour and technology intensive commodities. RCAs with product level detail within these broad categories have not been provided by the author even while it is stated that RCA identification at the aggregate level masks heterogeneity at the product level. For the last sub-period of 2000-2003, the author refers the readers to Batra and Khan, 2005 for product details/ commodity names. It is not clear, therefore, from Veeramani's analysis if within category gains and/or losses of comparative advantage are for the same commodities or if new commodities have contributed to the increase/decrease. As regards commodity groups, since the 1990s, India is observed to have gained comparative advantage in food items, chemicals, iron and steel, textiles and other manufactures. China retains high comparative advantage in textiles and improves in commodity groups like machinery and transport equipments and other manufactures and experiences a loss of comparative advantage for some commodities within the food items and chemicals commodity groups. Again, the individual product items with RCA greater than one in these commodity groups are not listed or provided by the author.

The observation on negligible change in the structure of comparative advantage for India and China over the period 2000-2003 in Batra and Khan (2005) is also made by Wignaraja (2011) in his analysis extended to the year 2009 at the HS-2 digit level. The analysis using WITS database is only for merchandise trade as data for services is not available. Taking Batra and Khan (2005) as reference analysis, the number of sectors for which India and China have comparative advantage in 2009 is found to be almost the same as in 2000 and 2003. In 2009 though, the number of sectors for which China has comparative advantage is 44 and more than the 37 sectors for which India holds comparative advantage. In particular in the medium and high technology sectors, China is in a relatively advantageous position vis-à-vis India. In the top 10 sectors with comparative advantage in 2009, the highest rank is enjoyed by sectors HS-46 (plaiting material) and HS-66 (umbrellas, walking sticks and seat sticks). Other prominent sectors are artificial flowers, human hair, headgear, textile, apparel, footwear and leather products. The top 10 sectors with comparative advantage for India are a mix of primary products, resource-based manufactures and some low technology manufactures. The sectors holding the top two positions are HS-71 (pearls, precious stones, metals and coins) and HS-50 (silk). These are followed by carpets, other textile floorings, cotton, lac, gum, vegetable textile fibres, paper yarn, woven fabric, ores, slag, ash, vegetable plaiting materials, vegetable products, other textiles, bird skin and feathers.

In the in-between year of 2006, at a very aggregate level of HS-1 classification Tian and Yu (2012) in a comparative analytical framework find India to have a greater degree of constancy in its comparative advantage structure relative to China. Using the standard measure, Tian and Yu report the value of the RCA index at the HS 1-digit level for the years 2000 and 2006 (Table 2.1). In 2000, China had a strong comparative advantage in sectors like textile and apparel, chemicals and plastics, leather, woods and paper, metal, foodstuffs and beverages. From among these sectors, in 2006, China continues to be comparatively advantageously placed in textile and apparel though with a reduced value of the index. In other sectors like chemicals and plastics, leather, woods and paper, metal, foodstuffs and beverages, China moves from an advantageous position to being disadvantageously placed in 2006. China, in 2006, enjoys comparative advantage in machinery, transport and equipment. In contrast, India in 2000 had a significant comparative advantage in industries such as metal, tobacco and mineral, and foodstuff and beverages. It continues to have comparative advantage in these industries, except for foodstuff and beverages. However, its competitiveness has weakened in the last decade partly because of the strong competition from China and other ASEAN countries (Yu, 2011). The RCA analysis with reference to the ASEAN economies is taken up in another section of this monograph.

Table 2.1

RCA Index: India and China

Code	*Description*	*China*		*India*	
		2000	*2006*	*2000*	*2006*
0	Animals & Vegetables	0.383	0.284	0.359	0.383
1	Foodstuff & Beverages	1.09	0.894	1.403	0.794
2	Tobacco & mineral	0.991	0.999	2.699	2.067
3	Chemicals & Plastics	1.356	0.877	0.593	0.585
4	Leather, Woods & Paper	1.307	0.945	0.664	0.586
5	Textile & Apparel	2.918	1.905	0.991	0.958
6	Footwear & Glass	0.287	0.17	0.097	0.12
7	Metals	1.24	0.867	2.891	1.995
8	Machinery & Transport Equipment	0.992	1.231	0.376	0.637
9	Miscellaneous Manufactures	0.522	0.829	0.38	0.346

Source: Tian and Yu, 2012.

2.1.2 India and China: Divergence in the Structure of RCA

While there may be little difference in the number of sectors with comparative advantage in the global market between India and China, the constituent number and nature of commodities with comparative advantage varies across sectors for the two economies. This is evident from the SRCC analysis undertaken by Batra and Khan, 2005 and in the more sophisticated analysis undertaken by Batra (2007) as also in the sector-wise identification of comparative advantage for the year 2009 undertaken by Wignaraja (2011). Batra and Khan (2005) calculate the SRC coefficient for RCA indices of manufactured products for India and China in the world market. Measuring thus the extent of similarity in comparative advantage, the analysis is an attempt to identify the degree of competition that the two economies pose to each other in the global market. For the manufacturing sector as a whole, India and China show no correlation and hence no competition. Within manufacturing, however, the two economies are competitive in sectors like organic chemicals, inorganic chemicals, that make a high demand for capital, skill, technology and scale; resource intensive sectors like non-metallic mineral manufactures, n.es. and manufactures of metals which is low in its demand for capital, skill, technology, and scale. In the road vehicles category, India and China enter into a competitive relationship in 2003 from a complementary relationship in 2000 (Table 2.2).

Table 2.2

Sectors where India and China Compete for Global Market Share

Factor Intensity	*SITC Code*	*Sector Description*	*SRCC*	*SRCC*
			2000	*2003*
IV	51	Organic chemicals	.02	.25***
IV	52	Inorganic chemicals	.11	.41**
I	66	Non-metallic mineral manufactures n.e.s	.06	.31
II	69	Manufactures of metals	.38*	.05

Note: UNCTAD classification: IV-high demand for capital, skill, technology and scale, II-low demand for capital, skill, technology and scale, I: labour and resource intensive.

*-significant at 1%, **significant at 5%, ***-significant at 10%.

Source: Batra and Khan, 2005.

In resource intensive categories like the textile yarns, fabric, made up articles, n.e.s and related products and articles of apparel and clothing accessories, India and China are in a complementary relationship (Table 2.3). Between 2000 and 2003, complementary relationship has evolved in sectors like photographic apparatus, equipment and supplies and optical goods n.e.s.; watches and clocks, and iron and steel; and lost in sectors like medicinal and pharmaceutical products and footwear.

Table 2.3

Sectors where India and China are Complementary in the Global Market

Factor Intensity	*SITC Code*	*Sector Description*	*SRCC 2000*	*SRCC 2003*
IV	54	Medicinal and pharmaceutical products	-.44	-
IV	65	Textiles yarn, fabrics and made up articles ne.s., and related products	-.02	-.10
III, IV	77	Electrical machinery, apparatus and appliances, n.e.s., and electrical parts thereof (including non electrical counterparts n.e.s., of electrical household type equipment.	-	-.08
I	84	Articles of apparel and clothing accessories	-.22**	-.09
I	85	Footwear	-.70**	—

Note and Source: Refer Table 2.2.

The extent of competition is re-examined by Batra (2007) using a more sophisticated analysis based on statistical tests of convergence and a long term trend analysis over the period 1995-2003. SRCC for all sectors and manufacturing as a whole is observed to be low or negative and statistically insignificant (Table 2.4). The lack of any correlation between the Indian and Chinese comparative advantage in the global market is further confirmed when the analysis is undertaken for individual commodities classified according to factor intensity.

Table 2.4

SRCC: India and China RCA: 1995-2003

Year	*Aggregate*	*Manufacturing*
1995	0.08**	0.07
2000	-0.01	0.01
2003	-0.02	-0.01

Notes: *, ** and *** represent significance at the 10, 5 and 1 per cent levels, respectively.

Source: Batra (2007).

Batra (2007) presents further evidence of the divergent structure of comparative advantage of India and China using the time trend analysis. The linear time trend statistic is negative and significant. This holds true at the aggregate level as well as for manufacturing, and in both global and ASEAN markets. The increasing divergence in the comparative advantage of the two economies is also evident from results of the Daniels test[9] which is a counterpart to the more conventional parametric testing for trend by OLS (ordinary least squares) regression. The coefficients are again negative and significant for both the global and ASEAN markets at the aggregate and manufacturing sector levels.

Evidence of divergent structures of comparative advantage in the year 2009 is also indicated in the examples provided by Wignaraja (2011). The high technology manufactured product like electronic goods while having moved up the ranking of sectors with comparative advantage enjoyed by China, does not figure in the sectors where India enjoys comparative advantage in the global market. Even for sectors where there is an overlapping advantage for India and China, the latter holds a far larger share of the world market in comparison with India. This, in fact, is true for China even in case of sectors for which the ranking has slipped to a lower position like in case of railway products and equipment (Table 2.5).

Rana and Dowling (2008) have calculated the RCA for India and China relative to South Asia and East Asia respectively over the period 1993-2004. In 2004, South Asia has comparative advantage primarily in primary goods and labour intensive manufactures. Both in 1993 and 2004, textiles, yarn and fabric, clothing and accessories show the maximum comparative advantage. The commodity categories that have moved from disadvantage to advantage over the reference time period include petroleum and petroleum products, metal manufactures, organic chemicals, vegetable oils, miscellaneous manufactures and iron and steel. The structure of comparative

9. Given a time series yt, the Daniels Test calculates Pearson's correlation coefficient between corresponding ranks R(yt) and a time trend. The use of ranks makes the test robust against outliers. Also, the test does not assume normality in the analysed data or any particular trend pattern, such as a linear trend.

advantage remains largely similar over the two reference time points with the top 25 constituent commodity categories having a majority of items common over the time points. The authors also calculate the SRCC for RCA structure in 1993 and 2004. The coefficient of SRC is found to be high for most countries in South Asia including India which has the highest SRCC of .85 in the region. Bangladesh shows the maximum change in the region with a SRCC of .55. In contrast PRC in East Asia has the lowest SRCC showing maximum change

Table 2.5

Top 10 Sectors with Comparative Advantage: India and China, 2009

India			*China*		
HS Code	*Sector Description*	*World Market Share*	*HS Code*	*Sector Description*	*World Market Share*
71	Pearls, precious stones, metals, coins etc	10.2	46	Manufactures of plaiting material, basketwork, etc.	71.2
50	Silk	9.8	66	Umbrellas, walking sticks, seat sticks, whips etc.	70.1
57	Carpets and other textile floor coverings	8.5	67	Bird skin, feathers, artificial flowers, human hair etc.	62.9
52	Cotton	7.7	50	Silk	46.4
13	Lac, gums, resins, vegetable saps, and extracts nex	8.4	65	Headgear and parts thereof	42
53	Vegetable textiles fibres nes, paper yarn, woven fabric	6.5	63	Other made textiles articles, sets, worn clothing etc.	40
26	Ores, slag and ash	5	61	Articles of apparel, accessories, knit or crochet	33.7
14	Vegetable plaiting material, vegetable products nes	5.1	64	Footwear, gaiters, and the like and parts thereof	33.6
63	Other made textiles articles, sets, worn clothing etc.	5.5	58	Special woven or tufted fabric, lace, tapestry etc	34.6
67	Bird skin, feathers, artificial flowers, human hair etc.	5.1	42	Articles of leather, animal gut, harness, travel goods	35.3

Source: Wignraja, 2011.

in the structure of its comparative advantage relative to the other countries in the region. Significant change is observed in the RCA of primary goods for People's Republic of China (PRC) with some commodities experiencing a move from advantage to disadvantage in the primary goods sector between 1993 and 2004. For RCAs of manufactured sector commodities such as telecom and sound equipment, metal manufactures, pre-fabricated fittings, electrical machinery parts and office machines, PRC shows an improvement.

Raychaudhuri *et al.* (2003) in an earlier study on trade patterns for South Asia have calculated the RCA for India using the Balassa index. Changes in RCA for India, Sri Lanka, and Bangladesh over the 1990s for a select group of exports to the EU and US markets are reported. In general, it is indicated that trade in the region is characterised by declining RCA in many traditional export items and specifically, that, in rubber, tyres and tubes India has no RCA in the EU market, but a stable RCA in the US market. In man-made fabrics, on the other hand, it has an increasing RCA in EU market in the 1990s but no RCA in the US market. For outwear as for undergarments, India has gained comparative advantage in the 1990s in the US market. The authors do not however specify the level of commodity disaggregation at which the RCA has been calculated or provide details of sector-wise/commodity-wise RCA calculations.

2.1.3 RCA and India's Competitiveness in Regional Markets

Extending the concept of similarity/divergence of the comparative advantage structure further, Batra (2007) uses the RCA to evaluate the extent of competition between India and China in the regional ASEAN market. The regional analysis is undertaken to examine the implications of the India-ASEAN FTA. India's FTA with ASEAN announced in 2003 was signed in 2009 and implemented in 2010. China had an effective free trade area with ASEAN as of 1 January 2010. Batra (2007) is the first study to undertake an assessment of the extent of competitive threat from China for India in the ASEAN market using the RCA index and market share analysis. The analysis has been undertaken using the Lall and Albaladejo (2003) methodology of identifying threat outcomes based on relative changes in market shares of the two countries. The threat outcomes classified as direct threat, partial threat, and no threat are examined for the best performing sectors and commodities for India and China in the ASEAN market.

Interestingly among the top 10 sectors where India enjoys comparative advantage in ASEAN there is no sector-wise overlap with China. Irrespective of the RCA ranking, there are 25 sectors where India and China, both, enjoy comparative advantage in the ASEAN market. China has a distinct advantage in terms of higher RCAs in 12 of these sectors. In the remaining 13, India is either equally or relatively advantageously placed in the ASEAN market. However, despite this equal or more advantage, India is considered likely to be overtaken in these sectors given China's prior entry on a preferential basis owing to the China-ASEAN FTA (CAFTA). Of these, 5 sectors are India's best performing sectors though not so for China.[10]

At the commodity level, threat identification has been undertaken using RCA as well as market share analysis. Of the top 10 sectors, 8 sectors have the maximum number of commodities where China and India enjoy comparative advantage in the ASEAN market. Among these, 50 commodities are such that India and China enjoy equal comparative advantage. Examined for threat perception, a majority of these commodities are such that while India and China have both experienced an increase in market share in ASEAN, China's share has doubled, so that India faces a partial threat in these commodities. China poses a partial threat for a greater number of commodities in sectors: HS-55 (manmade staple fibres), HS-82 (tools, implements, cutlery etc of base metal) and HS-84 (nuclear reactors, boilers, machinery etc). In HS-52 (cotton), India and China pose a partial threat to each other for an equal number of commodities. In sector HS-73 (articles of iron or steel), India faces a direct threat from China in three commodities: fittings (pipe or tube, of non-malleable cast iron), flanges (stainless steel) and needles (sewing, darning or embroidery, iron or steel) and partial threat in one (switch blades, crossing frogs, point rods and other crossing pieces (iron or steel),

---

10. For a detailed list of sectors see Batra, 2007

while itself posing a partial threat to China for two commodities: articulated link chain other than roller chain (of iron or steel) and springs and leaves for springs (of iron or steel). In HS-85 (electrical and electronic equipment), India poses a partial threat to China for sound signalling equipment and faces a direct threat from China in the case of insulating fittings for electrical machine appliances and equipment. India faces a direct threat from China and vice versa for some commodities across the 8 sectors. In each sector, the number of commodities directly threatened by China's exports is small. The list of commodities with their threat outcomes in sectors facing maximum competitive threat is presented in Table 2.6.

Table 2.6

Commodity-level Competition[a] between India and China in ASEAN

HS Code	*Sector Description*	*No. of Commodities*	*Threat*		
			Direct	*None[b]*	*Partial[c]*
29	Organic chemicals	11	1	1[d]	9 (4,2)
52	Cotton	7	1	1	3 (1,1)
55	Manmade staple fibres	5	0	1	4 (1,3)
61	Articles of apparel, accessories, knit or crochet	2	—	2	—
73	Articles of iron or steel	6	3	0	3 (2,1)
82	Tools, implements, cutlery, etc. of base metal	4	2	1	1 (0,1)
84	Nuclear reactors, boilers, machinery etc.	13	3	2	8 (1,3)
85	Electrical, electronic equipment	2	1	0	1 (1,0)

Notes: a: Indicated by the number of commodities that face the respective threat outcome; b: no threat for India/China under threat; c: increase in one country's share is twice or more than that for the other (India, China) (outside the parentheses is the number of commodities for which both countries experience an increase in share); d: increase is marginal.

HS: harmonised system of commodity classification.

Source: Batra, 2007

Apart from the sectors with maximum comparative advantage, Batra (2007) also examines the threat posed by China to India in the ASEAN for all commodities for which India enjoys comparative advantage in the ASEAN market. Further, the author proceeds to identify commodities for which India poses partial threat to China in the ASEAN market and classifies these as those with potential for a threat, that is, an implicit threat as termed by Batra, 2007. The potential for these commodities to overtake the Indian comparative advantage in ASEAN arises from the fact that even though India and China are both advantageously placed in the ASEAN market and India has a greater market share in ASEAN, China's prior preferential entry in ASEAN may allow it to overtake India. India's market share may well fall by the time India is able to make a preferential entry through its FTA with the ASEAN.

Shinoj and Mathur (2008) undertake an analysis of India's comparative advantage in exports of major agricultural commodities with respect to Asia and compare it with that of other major Asian exporters. Ten major agricultural commodities/commodity groups including tea, coffee, rice, spices, cashew, oil meals, fresh fruits, fresh vegetables, meat and meat preparations, and marine products have been selected for the analysis, based on their respective shares in India's total agricultural exports. During the period under study (1991-2004), these commodities together accounted for more than 65 per cent of India's total agricultural export earnings from the world. The comparative advantage for these commodities, in correspondence with the SITC classification, is calculated using exports data as from the FAO Trade Yearbook and the index of symmetric comparative advantage (RSCA). The study reveals that exports of various agricultural commodities from India have responded differently in terms of comparative advantage during the post-reforms period. India has enjoyed a comparative advantage in tea exports but has depicted a declining trend over the years. However, Sri Lanka has shown a far better advantage in comparison to India and other countries like China and Indonesia. A similar pattern has been observed in coffee exports also, where India has been found losing its comparative advantage to other coffee exporters like Vietnam and Indonesia. An unstable pattern of comparative advantage has been observed in case of rice exports with intermittent ups and downs in the status. A gradual decline in India's comparative advantage has been depicted for exports of spices and cashew also. Vietnam has bypassed India in the later years in terms of comparative advantage in cashew exports. As opposed to other commodities, India has strengthened its position in the global markets in exports of oil meals. But as far as the exports of fresh fruits and fresh vegetables are concerned, India cannot boast to have a comparative advantage. While Philippines and Turkey have dominated in fresh fruits exports, Israel has been dominant in the exports of fresh vegetables. India's status in exports of meat and its preparations and marine products has not been very comfortable. Although marine products dominate India's agricultural exports, it cannot be attributed to India's comparative advantage in the global markets. It is assumed to be more due to a growing demand for these products among the international consumers. In nut shell, India's comparative advantage in most of the important agricultural exports has been found to be eroding and in certain commodities, losing out to other Asian competitors, during the period after economic reforms.

Bhattacharyya (2011) has evaluated India's comparative advantage in three broad categories of horticultural exports—vegetables, fruits, and flowers, relative to the South East/East Asian countries of Thailand, Malaysia, Indonesia and China in a diverse set of markets of Asian, North American and EU countries. Calculating the RCA for the year 2009 using the Balassa index, the author finds that as regards vegetables, India has a significant comparative advantage over China, Thailand, Malaysia and Indonesia in European and North American markets. In the Asian market however, China and Malaysia have an advantage over India. Indian's comparative advantage over China, Thailand, Malaysia, and Indonesia in the fruits market of Europe is significant. Whereas in the Asian market, India stands at a disadvantage compared to all these countries. Also, China and Malaysia have a comparative advantage over India in the North American market for fruits. In case of flower market, India enjoys comparative advantage both in the markets of Europe and that of North America. In the Asian market, both Malaysia and Indonesia have a comparative advantage over India.

2.1..4 Re-evaluation of RCA: Fragmented Production, Value Addition and Global Imbalances

The global financial crisis and the associated global imbalances have led to a re-assessment of trade surplus and deficit across nations with implications for the thus far followed formulations of comparative advantage based on the existing trade patterns of a country. A brief exposition of the emerging research in this context is presented below.

Globalisation, lowering of trade barriers and the information and communications technology induced lowering of transportation costs have led to a dilution of physical borders for economic transactions. Production processes have as a consequence been spliced across national borders leading to the emergence of global and regional supply chains. Significantly, as supply chain led trade increases in magnitude, the assessment of the value of exports from any one country tends to get more and more distorted. Given the large import content of exports, it may not be correct to take the value of exports as the value addition by any country in a product category. With the emergence and evolution of global supply chains wherein the production processes have got spliced across borders, attributing the full value of a product to a country from which it is exported to its final consumption destination may exaggerate the value addition as also mislead with regard to comparative advantage of the exporting country. The problem of multiple counting of certain value added components in the official trade statistics suggests that the traditional measure of RCA may distort the actual ranking of competitiveness among countries.

It is also noteworthy that in these supply chains emerging market economies have been observed to be downstream with relatively larger imported content in their exports. Further, the Asian supply chain is more dispersed and in comparison with the developed country participation in the supply chain where goods are directly imported from the hub country, in case of Asian supply chain, goods that enter as inputs into the final goods cross national borders including that of the hub several times (Bayoumi, 2011). The re-evaluation of the RCA may therefore be more revealing in case of the emerging market economies. Some of these 'revelations' are discussed below.

Koopman *et al.*, 2013 have shown that using gross exports data India has a strong RCA in finished metal products and ranks fourth in a sample of 26 countries. However on accounting for imported content and estimating RCA on the basis of domestic value addition, India's advantage in this sector is converted into a disadvantage and the ranking for the RCA index changes to 15th. Interestingly, it is also observed that in case of China accounting of foreign/imported content of export commodities shows that sectors that are more sophisticated or high skilled like computers, electronic devices, and telecommunication equipment tend to have notably lower share of domestic content. Conversely this implies that China's own value addition/comparative advantage in these sectors is not as distinct as is evident on the basis of RCA calculations using the traditional Balassa index (Koopman *et al.*, 2013).

Global value chains have thus made imperative that the export value statistics be re-evaluated for domestic value addition content. This development has some relevant implications for the Chinese contribution to global trade and in a related manner with the US trade deficit. Wei (2012) in his analysis of the US-China trade and investment relationship states that the standard trade statistics exaggerate the true exports of value added from China to the US as any product that is exported from China may have only a small proportion of value addition taking place in China while using many components from other countries and maybe having been designed in the US. So that even though a product is exported from China, it may not be the entire value of the product that can be accounted for in China. There may be other sources of value addition that are subsumed when a product value is identified with the country of export. The point is made by Wei in referring to the Chinese trade surplus vis-à-vis the US. The fact that Chinese goods commonly have embedded components from other countries and while this may be true to a much lesser extent for the US, implies that the stated Chinese surplus against the US may actually be smaller (by 40% according to estimates provided by Wei, 2012) in value added terms.

According to Wei, there are several examples of discrepancy between gross and value added trade to be found in case studies of global value chains in sectors like electronics, apparel, and motor vehicles.

In an interesting use of the Balassa RCA index, the paper by Barattieri (2011), aimed at providing an explanation for the emergence of global imbalances, empirically establishes the emergence of a systematic negative relationship, starting in the mid-1990s, between specialisation in export of services and current account for a set of 85 OECD and developing countries including India. The RCA is calculated for services and goods with an aggregate perspective, and hence essentially for two goods. The calculations show India to be an exception along with Ireland as a country having become increasingly specialised in the export of services only in recent times. In a scatter plot of current account to GDP and the RCA in services that the author does for the OECD and BRICS countries, evidence shows a strong negative relationship between RCA and current account in 2006 while the same is absent in 1995. The conclusion is reinforced when a regression with current account to GDP as dependent variable is undertaken for the same set of countries for reference years 1995 and 2006. The result is robust in a cross section and panel estimation as also after controlling for other determinants of current account. Taking the analysis forward, the author develops a theoretical model to explain the channels through which the interaction between comparative advantage and asymmetric trade liberalisation can explain the current account deficits and hence the global imbalances that have also been considered to be at the base of the recent global financial crisis. Disaggregating the trade balance into its two components—goods trade and services, the author develops a model theorising the interplay between the RCA and observed asymmetric liberalisation in manufacturing and services trade liberalisation to explain the US trade deficit. However, India is not a part of the linkage analysis which is hence not discussed here. Of relevance here is the usage of the concept of RCA to explain the emergence of trade deficit in the US or conversely surplus in the Chinese economy among other surplus economies.

2.1.5 RCA and Networked Production: Relative Placement of India and China

Further, as global trade increased and incomes converged, trade has increasingly been in the nature of intra-industry trade especially in products from the manufacture, chemicals and machinery category. Intra-industry trade has increased for countries that are well integrated in the global supply chain, China being one of the major countries in this respect. Rapidly growing trade and networked production and trade has thus marked the emergence of some emerging economies such as China as significant trade partners.

The global supply chains have also increased the possibility of increased technological content of the emerging market economies' exports. The contribution of high technology and medium technology exports such as machinery and transport equipment to world exports has increased while that of lower technology like textiles has declined. Countries that invest in technology enhancing policies even if it is adaptation of imported technology or through FDI (foreign direct invetsment) may be able to create comparative advantage relative to countries with similar factor endowments (Lall, 2000). It has been reported (Bayoumi, 2011) that in case of China the imported content of Chinese high technology goods is very high and this increased by almost 30 per cent between 1995 and 2008. But when adjusted for foreign content it is much lower (24%). Adjusting exports to exclude foreign content and to more clearly account for domestic value addition thus reveals a different picture in this context too.

Ferrarini and Scaramozzino (2012) have used the idea of comparative advantage to present a country's position in the production network and consequently evaluate its ability to integrate itself at different probable levels of value addition in the production chain. The analysis makes use of a measure of comparative advantage based on net trade flows. It further uses the Lafay index that is related to the Grubel-Lloyd index of intra-industry trade to examine the product space. Traditional RCA index uses export flows as export specialisation is seen as the most reliable indicator of a country's underlying capabilities as per traditional theory according to which trade specialisation is directly related to resource endowments and to available technology. In the Ferrarini and Scaramozzino analysis, comparative advantage is measured using net trade flows to more appropriately indicate actual production capabilities of a country and also as more relevant in a world of production networks and global production sharing. Exports and imports could reflect differential information on production capabilities of a country. Additional to the net trade flows based RCA, a measure of capabilities is defined as the Lafay index which is the distribution of normalised trade balances (that is the inverse of Grubel Lloyd index) of a country among its products weighed by the sectoral contribution to the trade balance. The analysis is undertaken among other countries for India and for average trade flows on 2006-07. Balassa and Lafay index present a diverse picture of specialisation for India. The former reveals India to have specialisation in the first and third quartiles of productivity (sum of the product of RCA index and average income level of a country) with presence also in the highest quartile. The latter index shows that India is over represented in the lowest quartile of productivity distribution, while it also has a strong presence in the upper quartiles and has already established a specialisation profile in the top half of the product space. Product space is taken as a critical variable in identifying the developmental prospects of a country as it is calculated based on the proximity of the index of specialisation of two products, which in turn captures the closeness of two commodities in the product space in terms of the profile of their joint RCA. Proximity is a reflection of the ability to adapt to new sectors. No clear conclusion can therefore be drawn from Ferrarini and Scaramozzino analysis on India's ability to connect with different product groups in a fragmented product space.

Fung *et al.* (2013) make an interesting presentation of the relative places that India and China occupy in the global and regional production networks using the RCA index. Giving an understanding of the placement of the two economies in international production networks Fung *et al.* state that in 2010, 28.4 per cent of China's total trade was in parts and components having increased from 22 per cent in 2000. In comparison, India's trade in parts and components has a share of 12.4 per cent in its total trade having declined from 17.2

per cent in 2000. While a reflection of the growing total exports of India, the statistics also reflect India's relative smaller participation in the parts and components trade. In absolute terms China's exports of parts and components are almost 15 times those of India (Fung *et al.*, 2013). Further, the Chinese trade of parts and components according to Fung *et al.* is asymmetric in terms of the imports being majorly from the East Asia and Pacific region and the exports getting distributed across the EU, North America and East Asia and Pacific. In contrast, India's parts and components trade draws imports from the East Asia and Pacific while its major export destinations are the NAFTA and EU economies. South Asia accounts for less than one per cent of India's parts and components trade. Between India and China, telecom equipment and textiles and yarn are the largest exports of parts and components from China to India, and in the reverse flow textile yarn, fabrics, and made-up materials dominate over the reference period. Overall in the parts and components trade, China exports and imports mostly electronic related intermediate goods while India exports materials related to the textile and clothing network and imports ICT (information and communications technology) related parts. This presentation of facts has been supported by a formal RCA analysis in the Fung *et al.* study for China and Greater China[11] versus India and South Asia. The standard Balassa index is used for identifying the structure of comparative advantage. In 2010, in India, only 10 items comprising 13.3 per cent of its exports of parts and components have RCA greater than one in comparison with 38 in China that constitute 50.7 per cent of its exports of parts and components. Fung *et al.* also calculate the RCA of imports and show that 28 per cent of China's imports of parts and components and 21.3 per cent of India's imports of parts and components have RCA greater than one. The authors interpret these calculations to imply that China has comparative advantage in production operations and India has comparative advantage in assembly operations (Table 2.7).

---

11. Greater China includes Hong Kong, Macau, Taiwan

2.1.6 RCA and Regional Economic Integration between South and Southeast Asia

Regional economic integration process between South and Southeast Asia is essentially led by the formal initiative of a PTA (preferential trading arrangement) between India and the 10 member regional organisation, the ASEAN as also through India's participation in the East Asia Summit (EAS) that was established in 2005. China's announcement for an FTA with ASEAN in 2001 triggered a series of similar announcements by other regional economies including India. For India this is a further consolidation of its Look East Policy that was initiated in 1991-92 with the aim of drawing lessons on economic liberalisation and export promotion from the ASEAN economies. In the 2000s, this association was given a new dimension of regionalism. The announcement towards an EHP as part of the India-ASEAN FTA was made in 2003. The FTA was signed in 2009 and implemented in 2010. The EAS visualised and proposed the idea of the formation of a Pan Asian integration framework in the nature of an Asian economic community that would include the 16 member economies of ASEAN, China, Japan, Korea, Australia, New Zealand, and India, each of which has an FTA agreement with ASEAN. ASEAN is an existing regional organisation/trade bloc that has been accepted as the nucleus of the proposed Asian economic community. With the centre of gravity of the global economy shifting to the east, the rise of India along with China has been in the spotlight and both economies have come to be regarded as opportunities for economic alliances with potential for economic growth. Influenced by these developments, comparisons between India and China have been part of the analysis on Asian economic integration.

Economic integration through FTAs is theoretically considered as a second best option vis-à-vis the first best option of multilateral liberalisation. However, multilateral agreements while involving progressive liberalisation have over the recent years become more and more tedious and protracted with the required consensus becoming increasingly difficult to achieve owing to the large worldwide participation in the negotiation process at the WTO. RTAs are beneficial as given the fewer number of member countries, negotiations are easier and agreement on diverse issues may be achievable. This allows for an expanded scope and coverage in the RTAs in comparison with what may be possible in the multilateral negotiations. In their simplest forms, RTAs remove tariffs on intra-bloc trade in goods. Many, though, go beyond to cover NTBs (non-tariff barriers) and extend liberalisation to investment and services. In their deepest forms, these agreements aim at becoming an economic union involving the establishment of common executive, judicial and legislative institutions (Schiff and Winters, 2003). The benefits of RTAs, though, need to be carefully weighed against the distortions that are a consequence of the inherently discriminatory nature of these FTAs.

Table 2.7

Comparison of Comparative Advantage in Parts and Components Trade*

Country/Group		*Exports Production Operations*		*Imports Assembly Operations*	
		No. of Products	*% of Products*	*No. of Products*	*% of Products*
Greater China	Total Greater China	38	50.7	26	34.7
	China	38	50.7	21	28
	Hong Kong	23	30.7	23	30.7
	Taiwan	26	34.7	16	21.3
South Asia	Total South Asia	10	13.3	17	22.7
	India	10	13.3	16	21.3
	Pakistan	4	5.3	10	13.3
	Sri Lanka	5	6.7	18	24

Note: *RCA>1.

Source: Fung *et al.*, 2013.

Traditional trade theory, following Viner (1950), identifies the welfare implications of RTAs in terms of trade creation and/or trade diversion. Trade creation refers to making available cheaper products from member countries as substitutes for more expensive domestic production, while trade diversion occurs if imports thus made are substitutes for more efficiently produced, extra bloc imports. A primary concern therefore is whether the PTA implies any efficiency cost and, as a consequence, undermines trade liberalisation through the multilateral process. Given that a PTA accords preferential treatment to members vis-à-vis non-members, there is always a possibility of trade being diverted away from non-members to members. On occasion when non-members are more efficient producers, this process of trade diversion will imply a cost in terms of denying both the producers' and the consumers' access to lower cost and more efficiently produced goods. A PTA, therefore, needs to be evaluated to determine if there are efficiency costs by way of distortion in the patterns of trade away from those expected on the basis of comparative advantage.

Batra (2006) attempts the dual task of evaluating the most efficient approach to the formation of a regional integration initiative between India and ASEAN as also taking on the apparent contradiction between PTAs and the multilateral trading system using the revealed comparative advantage methodology. From the Indian perspective the efficiency analysis is undertaken defining Asia as ASEAN+4, i.e., the ASEAN+3 economies and India. The fact that there was no prior analysis on the efficient sequencing of such an arrangement among a set of diverse economies and that any arrangement makes possible the creation as well as diversion of trade made it imperative that a cost analysis be undertaken to ascertain the most efficient approach towards regional economic integration in Asia. Batra (2006) makes an attempt to analyse the efficiency costs of two alternative approaches for regional integration in Asia. These are the ASEAN+3+1 or the convergence of individual ASEAN+1s. The former initiative implies India as the last entrant to a prior formation of the ASEAN+3 and the latter a convergence of the individual PTAs that each of the +4 economies has with ASEAN. Efforts at integration of the ASEAN+3 economies were accelerated in the post 1997-98 East Asian crisis. The 16 members of the EAS are now negotiating the RCEP (regional comprehensive economic partnership) agreement where the timing of accession is left open to individual members as per their readiness to adopt the constituent provisions. The RCEP is taken up for discussion in a subsequent section on gravity model analysis of regional trading agreements and the Pan Asian integration initiatives.

The analysis is undertaken using the RCA index and the regional orientation index. Efficiency costs are implied if in the wake of the FTA exports an economy gets increasingly oriented towards the ASEAN/ASEAN+4 market even if the individual economies do not enjoy comparative advantage in the exported products. Essentially the analysis examines whether the direction of exports under the new/proposed alternative is in contradiction with that which is based on existing comparative advantage or in other words the extent of trade distortion on account of the new regional trade formation. Costs are indicated in terms of the number of sectors for which exports to ASEAN are increasing but where the country does not have a comparative advantage. The change in regional orientation of exports is measured over the period 1995 and 2004. The analysis is undertaken at the HS-2 digit classification of export products for all FTA partners of ASEAN in the new configuration. The efficiency costs are observed to be lower for ASEAN relative to ASEAN+4 for all the economies except Japan. For China, the cost of alignment with ASEAN is low relative to alignment with ASEAN+4 and lowest among the +4 economies. In comparison with about 67 per cent for ASEAN+4, only 26 per cent sectors are such that despite being comparatively disadvantageously placed in the world market, China's exports from these sectors are getting increasingly oriented towards ASEAN. For India, in about 50 per cent of the sectors increased export orientation towards ASEAN is observed despite a lack of comparative advantage in the world market in comparison with 54 per cent such sectors in case of ASEAN+4. Corresponding figures for Korea are 68 and 78 per cent for ASEAN and ASEAN+4 respectively. Clearly, the ASEAN+1 arrangement is more cost efficient for all the +4 economies except Japan.

The efficiency costs of regionalism versus multilateralism is examined by making a comparison of the structure of comparative advantage for each of the +4 economies in the ASEAN/ASEAN+4 and world market. Greater the similarity in the RCA structure at the regional and multilateral level, lower would be the efficiency costs of alignment with the regional economies in a trading arrangement. A similar analysis is also undertaken for the comparative advantage structure in terms of factor intensity to examine the possible movement of factors between industries as production would be reoriented to match the changing demand on account of the preferential trading patterns. The alignment of the regional and global RCAs at the 6-digit level of HS classification has been checked using the SRCC at the aggregate level (for all sectors) and separately for agriculture, manufacturing, minerals and fuels, chemicals and plastics and manufactures chiefly by materials and miscellaneous manufactures. As evident from the results shown in Table 2.8, for India and the other economies, at the aggregate and individual sector level, the SRCC implies no significant costs for either of the ASEAN+1s or ASEAN+4 arrangements, even though the extent of alignment is slightly greater for the ASEAN+4 market.

Table 2.8

Alignment of Comparative Advantage vis-à-vis Multilateral Liberalisation

	India	*China*	*Japan*	*Korea*
All Sectors	0.66	0.72	0.73	0.63
	0.73	*0.84*	*0.79*	*0.78*
Agriculture & Allied	0.63	0.6	0.59	0.55
	0.74	*0.81*	*0.67*	*0.74*
Manufacturing	0.67	0.74	0.72	0.63
	0.73	*0.85*	*0.78*	*0.78*
Minerals & mineral fuels	0.64	0.44	0.68	0.48
	0.82	*0.85*	*0.89*	*0.78*
Chemicals & Plastics	0.7	0.75	0.65	0.67
	0.75	*0.86*	*0.73*	*0.82*
Manufactures chiefly by material	0.69	0.74	0.71	0.61
	0.74	*0.83*	*0.79*	*0.77*
Machinery	0.55	0.72	0.76	0.65
	0.57	*0.82*	*0.84*	*0.79*
Misc.(HS-90-99)	0.38	0.85	0.73	0.6
	0.5	*0.85*	*0.82*	*0.75*

Note: Figures italicised: ASEAN+4.
High:=/>0.8; modest: 0.5-0.7; low: .0-0.4. All significant.

Source: Batra, 2006.

In the factor intensity analysis the RCAs are re-classified according to five categories-primary, unskilled labour intensive, natural resource intensive, human capital intensive and technology intensive. A comparison of the RCA structure across these five categories and for ASEAN, ASEAN+4 and world market shows (Table 2.9) that for India the value of the SRCC is almost the same in the two target markets and hence there is no cost differential between aligning in the ASEAN+1 mode or in the ASEAN+3+1 mode. For the +3 economies, however, the ASEAN+3+1 mode is marginally more efficient. The difference in the costs of alignment through the ASEAN+3+1 and the ASEAN+1s is now both apparent and relevant.

In a further examination of the efficiency of formation of the regional trading arrangements, Batra (2006) calculates the extent of overlap between the existing and potential RCA structures of the +4 economies. The overlap is an indication of the scope for competition that each economy is likely to face in the target markets if the preferential agreements come into force. The potential competition is indicated by the global comparative advantage as it is considered likely that comparative advantage in the regional context would be easier to

Table 2.9

Alignment of Comparative Advantage and Shifts in Factor Intensity

	India	*China*	*Japan*	*Korea*
Human Capital Intensive	0.71	0.74	0.72	0.65
	0.75	*0.82*	*0.79*	*0.78*
Primary	0.65	0.55	0.62	0.57
	0.77	*0.82*	*0.77*	*0.79*
Unskilled Labour Intensive	0.62	0.66	0.71	0.6
	0.68	*0.75*	*0.78*	*0.75*
Natural Resource Intensive	0.71	0.62	0.75	0.6
	0.75	*0.77*	*0.8*	*0.77*
Technology Intensive	0.64	0.72	0.71	0.66
	0.67	*0.85*	*0.79*	*0.81*

Notes: Figures italicised: ASEAN+4.

High: 0.8 & above; modest: 0.5-0.7; low: .0-0.4. All significant.

Source: Batra, 2006.

develop in these commodities where prior global advantage exists. Maximum overlap of existing comparative advantage and hence maximum competition in the ASEAN market is observed between India and China. However, for 52 per cent of the commodities where India and China have an advantage in the world market as well as in ASEAN, India enjoys greater comparative advantage relative to China in the ASEAN market. Indian exports of these commodities are likely to be adversely affected if China makes a prior entry in ASEAN. Trade will be diverted away from India. Further, for 72 per cent of these commodities, India is actually more competitive than China even in the world market. Among these are commodities like marine products (fish and mollusks) and leguminous vegetables that belong to sectors 1-8 (HS classification). Tariff concessions have been offered on these commodities under the Early Harvest Programme (EHP) of China's FTA with ASEAN. India is, therefore, negatively affected through trade diversion on account of the implementation of the EHP of China's FTA with ASEAN. In the longer run when the ASEAN-China FTA is fully implemented, the maximum number of products that are likely to suffer export diversion belongs to the cotton sector. Commodities like cotton sewing thread, plain weave cotton, cotton yarn, twill weave cotton, and woven fabric of cotton may suffer maximum export diversion. The advantage that China may get on account of an FTA may render it cheaper for ASEAN to import these commodities from China, in which case there is trade diversion from India and in addition efficiency loss for ASEAN. This implies that there is a cost to staying out of the ASEAN arrangement for India on account of China's pre-emptive entry in ASEAN. As the threat of export diversion for India is evidently the highest from China, the potential for overlap of comparative advantage is analysed for India vis-à-vis China only. The set is defined as commodities that ASEAN imports and where India currently enjoys comparative advantage in the world market and is either more or equally advantageously placed relative to China. It is interesting to note that even though at present China is not as advantageously placed in the world market as India, it is the main source of ASEAN imports. In these commodities India has a potential for developing comparative advantage in ASEAN as it is already far more advantageously placed than China in the world market. A set of 19 such commodities is identified. Of these 19 commodities, 7 or 37 per cent belong to product groups like textiles, man-made filaments and foot wears and gaiters that are intensive in unskilled labour. The ASEAN-China FTA is expected to further intensify exports of these commodities from China to ASEAN and simultaneously prevent India from exploiting its potential for exports to ASEAN. China's entry in ASEAN prior to India through the ASEAN-China FTA thus also implies potential trade diversion for India.

The index of RCA has been calculated for India, ASEAN and China by Okamoto (2006) in the context of an evaluation of the FTAs that India and China have with the 10 member regional grouping. Whether the FTA is likely to be a beneficial arrangement for the two economies is the subject of Okamata's analysis. The policy question is explored in the light of the propositions expressed by Okamato that regional integration among developing countries often fails to lead to materialised expected benefits owing to little scope for intra or inter industry specialisation/trade as they tend to have similar comparative advantage structures (Langhammer and Heimenz, 1990). In the context, Okamoto examines if the trade structures of India, China, and ASEAN are complementary or competitive. In an exercise similar to Batra (2006), the RCA indices are calculated and then using the SRCC the extent of complementarity is determined. The RCA is however calculated at a more aggregate level of commodity specification, SITC-2 digit level. A positive and statistically significant value of the SRCC between the rankings of RCAs in ASEAN, China and, India is indicative of similarity and hence competitiveness among these countries. In such a case, there would be little scope for inter-industry trade/specialisation among the economies under consideration. In the opposite case of a negative and statistically significant value of the SRCC between the rankings of RCAs, the comparative advantage structures would be complementary and hence potentially beneficial if the economies were to participate in the FTA. Okamoto's findings reveal that Thailand and Philippines have a high, positive and statistically significant SRCC with India and China. An FTA between these economies would therefore not be gainful. India is in negotiations with Thailand for an FTA that though announced in 2003 has not progressed beyond the EHP with 84 commodities precisely for this reason. Domestic producers in India have been wary of the possible competition that cheaper imports from Thailand would introduce in India through the FTA. For the other economies—Indonesia, Malaysia and Singapore—Okamoto's results on the SRCC are statistically insignificant and hence indeterminate. India, though, has bilateral FTAs with all the three economies. The India-Singapore comprehensive economic cooperation agreement has generated trade as well as FDI for the two economies.

The analysis in the context of an India-ASEAN FTA has been undertaken by Chandran (2010) at a more detailed level. RCA is calculated for 8 ASEAN countries, 16 commodity groups and over the period 1990-2007. In the agricultural products group, the paper identifies scope for trade based on mean of RCAs between India and Brunei, Singapore and Cambodia. In the manufactured products category, scope for trade is identified in the resource-based iron and steel products from India. Similarly, the paper identifies the knowledge-based industry of chemical products as distinctly advantageous for India with possibilities of trade expansion. In the high technology industry of machinery and equipment, ASEAN has a relative advantage over India. Similarly in the electronics industry of integrated circuits and electronic components, the ASEAN countries Singapore, Thailand, Malaysia and Philippines have developed advantage over the reference period. In the labour intensive textiles and clothing sector, while India has a strong comparative advantage, so do some of the East Asian economies like Thailand and Indonesia, though with lower values of the RCA index. Additionally, with the phasing out of the MFA China is also likely to enter the competitive arena in this sector. In the face of the existing limited complementarity, it is necessary that India make the effort to further enhance its competence in the sector to face the possible competition from the ASEAN economies that is likely to emerge post MFA in the global market.

The RCA for the India, ASEAN, and China have also been calculated for the years 1998 and 2008 by Yu (2011). RCA index is calculated using the Balassa index and the SITC commodity classification. Analysing the data at SITC-1 digit level of classification, Yu shows that over the 1998 to 2008 decade, while China has retained its comparative advantage in miscellaneous manufactured goods, it has now acquired advantage in transport and equipment also. India's comparative advantage in the two reference years has however remained much the same, in sectors like food and live animals, crude materials, animal and vegetable oils, manufactured goods, and miscellaneous manufactured articles, with slight reduction in competitiveness owing to competition from countries like China (Yu, 2011).

Dasgupta *et al.* (2012) have evaluated the extent of trade complementarity between South and Southeast Asia using the RCA. The RCA is calculated at the 6-digit level and the results suggest strong complementarities between South and Southeast Asia. The categories of commodities where one or both countries enjoy comparative advantage cover 64 per cent of total trade or 2,843 product lines, indicating thereby strong potential for trade between the two regions. At a further level of detail, products with comparative advantage for South Asia include food, organic and inorganic material, textiles and metal products. Products where both regions enjoy comparative advantage but where South Asia is relatively more advantageously placed than east Asia includes yarn and textiles, apparel and other labour intensive goods like footwear, parts, jewellery. The growing complementarity between the two regions is attributable to the growing differences in factor endowments between the two regions (Shirotori *et al.*, 2009) as it is acknowledged that ultimately advantages derive from factor endowments and their changes over time. The analysis also shows that 47 per cent of South Asia's exports to China have both comparative advantage and a growing share in the Chinese market. The goods while indicating fair share of market penetration are mostly concentrated in industrial primary goods, with the exception of textiles (Dasgupta *et al.*, 2012).

ADB (2008) undertakes the estimation of complementarity and competitiveness among four south Asian economies, India, Bangladesh, Pakistan, and Sri Lanka, at the 5-digit SITC level. The estimation is undertaken over two time periods with average taken in each of these periods. The two reference time periods are 1991-1993 and 2004-06. The estimation over this time period is an attempt to examine if there has been any change in the structure of comparative advantage in correspondence with the changes that have occurred in these economies in the post economic liberalisation period. The study examines if the changes in production structures away from agriculture towards services sector are similarly reflected in the structure of comparative advantage also. The calculation is undertaken using the Balassa (1965) index of RCA. For each of the four countries, the study estimates a competitive basket by identifying goods for which it enjoys comparative advantage while the other three are not advantageously placed in these commodities. The average RCA is taken to be representative in each time period. On the basis of these calculations it is shown that the competitive basket has expanded for all four economies implying thus an expansion of the potential for intra-regional trade and hence the possibility of economic integration in South Asia. Significant expansion of the export basket is observed for India along with Sri Lanka. India is observed to have become more competitive relative to other SAARC economies in products like dyes, pharmaceuticals, yarn, etc. Product categories in which all four South Asian economies including India enjoy comparative advantage include commodities like textiles, shrimps, spices, woven carpets, cotton yarn wastes, etc.

As part of an analysis on South-South trade dynamics, Shirotori and Molina (2009) estimate the RCA for different developing sub-regions. The value of the RCA index is determined by comparing the weight of certain sectors in a country's export basket to that of a "reference group". Using the normalised approach to calculate the RCA index suggested by Laursen (1998), the normalised RCA index is measured based on the share of a product group, classified at the HS 4-digit level (covering 1,241 product groups), in a sub region's total exports to the South, relative to that of total South-South exports, the reference group for their study. When the value of the normalised index of a given product group is above 0 (and under or equal to 1), the sub region in question has a comparative advantage in that product group in relation to other sub regions included in South-South trade. The authors identify the frequency as the number of products with comparative advantage in a product group. South Asia appears as the second most important group in terms of frequency next to East Asia in South-South trade in both reference years 1995 and 2005. For South Asia the authors also indicate the acquisition of comparative advantage in new product groups in 2005 relative to 1995. This trend is attributed to the export diversification undertaken by the economies in South Asia. Further, the analysis also shows that for South Asia comparative advantage was largely in the labour intensive sectors such as base metal products, textiles and apparel articles and chemical and allied products. Over the reference period, South Asia along with East Asia has shown the highest degree of improvement in their comparative advantage, particularly in the manufacturing sector. South Asia also has a growing comparative advantage in a wide range of export products to the South. The sub region also shows an increase in the aggregate RCA (that is roughly indicative of the degree of RCA exhibited in a particular sector) for sectors like textiles and articles (particularly apparel articles), base metal products, machinery and allied chemical products in 2005 relative to 1995. The overall share of South Asia in total South-South trade though is small.

2.1.7 RCA in the Services Sector

Compared to goods trade statistics, service trade statistics are fraught with limitations. Langhammer (2004) cites three reasons for the doubts with regard to services trade data. One, services are often intangibles and thus defy border registration or escape reporting systems through BoPs (balance of payments) documentation. Two, the separation between services and goods is not as clear as BoPs statistics suggest. More often than not, they are joint products even when services are disembodied from goods and when stored electronically as a file as an alternative to be printed as a book, their final appearance is of dual nature. Three, BoPs statistics cover cross-border trade only. Other modes of supply, in particularly those via factor movements, are covered either by company surveys (commercial presence) or remain uncovered (movement of natural persons). It therefore becomes evident that any interpretation of RCA in service trade critically hinges upon the mode of supply of individual service sectors, in particular whether services are supplied by cross-border trade or by commercial presence. It is also noteworthy that services are not only supplied by cross-border trade (so-called mode of supply 1, for instance, via data, or document or voice transmission) but also by movement of the consumer to the producer (so-called mode of supply 2: consumption abroad) or by factor movements, for capital via commercial presence (mode of supply 3) and for labour via movement of natural persons (mode of supply 4). Any aggregate view on net exports of services supplied by all four modes may be misleading if there is no information on which mode of supply dominates. So RCA analysis for services trade may not be straightforwardly comparable with RCA analysis for goods trade. Furthermore, the SITC applies to goods only and there has been no readily comparable classification for services. There was also no internationally comparable data for services trade until the OECD secretariat released in 2002 a new publication presenting total trade in services broken down by partner country for 26 OECD member countries for the years 1999 and 2000 (OECD, 2002). The data are on BoP basis and cover mode 1 (cross border supply) and mode 2 (consumption abroad) transactions while reflecting only a small part of mode 3 (commercial presence) and mode 4 (presence of natural persons). India appears as a partner country in the OECD dataset.

Fourie and Fintel (2009) present a snapshot of country rankings of global service exporters using the Balassa index for the year 2005. Their analysis includes 147 countries, extending the dataset used in earlier literature by including developing and emerging market economies. The RCAs are examined for 10 sectors viz., transportation, travel, communication services, construction services, insurance services, financial services, computer and information services, royalties and licence fees, other business services, personal, cultural and recreational services, using data from the *UNCTAD Handbook of Statistics*. Variations to the original Balassa index are introduced in order to present a more nuanced understanding of the contribution of each sector to individual economies. In addition to the Balassa index for services sector, a second index is defined vis-à-vis all exports and a third alternative where service exports are weighted against GDP. While the second index gives the relative significance of service sector exports relative to total exports, the third RCA index does so vis-à-vis the country's GDP. In their analysis, India reveals a very strong RCA for the computer and information services ahead of countries like Ireland, Israel, UK, and Finland. Computer and information service exports are also revealed as an important sector of the Indian economy. China reveals little comparative advantage in service exports.

De and Raychaudhuri (2008) report that the RCA scores of India's services exports are favourable and are constantly rising, thereby indicating India's strong comparative advantage in services trade. Using the traditional Balassa index they show that India has achieved comparative advantage in financial, and computer and information services over the period 1991-2005, while having lost advantage in traditional sectors such as transport and travel services.

In an analysis of India's global trade integration, Kowalski and Diehl (2009) indicate the country's increasing RCA in the services sector. The value of the index of RCA is stated to have increased from 0.941 in 1994 to 1.427 in 2003. Over the same period, China's RCA index value in services is shown to have declined from 0.687 to 0.48. The authors also state that a detailed sectoral analysis shows India to have a distinct comparative advantage in computer and communication services. The findings are based on IMF (BoP) data but no details of computational methodology are provided. The authors do however acknowledge the limited nature of the data stating that the IMF BoP statistics are imperfect proxies of services trade via mode 4 and that the data used represents largely services traded internationally by the first and second mode of supply (mode 1 and mode 2).

3

Gravity Model

The gravity model for trade is analogous to the Newtonian physics function that describes the force of gravity. The model explains the flow of trade between a pair of countries as being proportional to their economic "mass" (national income) and inversely proportional to the distance between them.

The model has a lineage that goes back to Tinbergen (1962) and Poyhonen (1963), who specified the gravity model equation as follows:

$Trade_{ij} = \alpha\ (GDP_i . GDP_j)/Distance_{ij}$................(1)

Where,

$Trade_{ij}$ is the value of the bilateral trade between country i and j,
GDP_i and GDP_j are country i and j's respective national incomes,
$Distance_{ij}$ is a measure of the bilateral distance between the two countries, and
α is a constant of proportionality.

3.1 Theoretical Foundations and Developments

While the core gravity equation has been used for empirical analysis since the econometric studies of trade by Tinbergen (1962) and Poyhonen (1963), the theoretical foundations to the model are of more recent origin. The most classic and early application of the model to international trade was perhaps by Linnemann (1966). Trade theorists have found the model to be consistent with theories of trade based upon models of imperfect competition and with the Hecksher-Ohlin (H-O) model. Frankel (1997) credits Helpman and Krugman (1985) for the standard gravity model. The derivation of a proportionate relationship between trade flows and country size as given by Helpman do not include a role for distance. There are several reasons, though, for the inclusion of distance as an explanatory variable. These include taking distance as a proxy for transport costs, as an indicator of the time elapsed during shipment, relevant particularly for perishable goods in which case the probability of surviving intact is a decreasing function of time in transit, as a measure of synchronisation costs when factories combine multiple inputs and the timing of combining these needs to be synchronised so as to prevent emergence of bottlenecks and synchronisation costs increase with increasing distance. Distance may be correlated with the costs of searching for trading opportunities and the establishment of trust between potential trading partners, that is, transaction costs. It is also possible that greater geographical distance is correlated with larger cultural differences. Cultural differences can impede trade in many ways such as inhibiting communication, clashes in negotiating styles etc. Bergstrand's (1985) version of the imperfect substitutes theory incorporated a role for shipping costs, proxied in practice by distance.

More recently, Deardorff (1995) has derived the gravity model from H-O theory. Deardorff shows that the gravity model can be derived from two extreme cases of the classical framework of the H-O model. The first case is frictionless trade, in which the absence of all impediments to trade in homogenous products causes producers and consumers to be indifferent among trading partners. Resolving this indifference randomly expected trade flows correspond exactly to the simple frictionless gravity equation if preferences are identical and homothetic or if demands are uncorrelated with supply and they depart from that equation systematically when there are such correlations. The second case is that different countries produce distinct goods, as in the H-O model with complete specialisation. Expression for bilateral trade is derived, first with Cobb-Douglas preferences and then with CES preferences. Distance is included in the second of the two models. Trade theories based upon imperfect competition and the H-O model justify the inclusion of the core variables-income and distance. Most studies have, however, included additional variables to control for differences in geographic factors, historical ties and at times economic factors like the overall trade policy and exchange rate risk.

Taking logarithms of the gravity model equation as in (1) we get the linear form of the model and the corresponding estimable equation as:

$$\text{Log}(\text{Trade}_{ij}) = \alpha + \beta_1 \log(\text{GDP}_i.\text{GDP}_j) + \beta_2 \log(\text{distance}_{ij}) + u_{ij} \quad \text{.....(2)}$$

Where α, β_1 and β_2 are coefficients to be estimated. The error term captures any other shocks and chance events that may affect bilateral trade between the two countries.

Equation (2) is the core gravity model equation where bilateral trade is predicted to be a positive function of income and negative function of distance. While initially the model was proposed with no theoretical background, several theories have now been used to support the trade model. In fact from a relative scarcity of theoretical justification of the gravity equation there now exists a surfeit of choice, so that a theory that best describes the model may not be so easily identifiable. It may just be said that it is possible to derive the gravity equation from a variety of leading theories. However, the gravity model of international trade has a consistent record of success as an empirical tool. The elasticities of trade with respect to distance and income are observed to be consistently high, signed correctly and statistically significant in an equation that explains a reasonable proportion of cross-country variation in international trade.

3.2 Empirical Applications

Empirically the gravity model has been the most successful model to explain trade flows.[1] The exporter GDP (gross domestic product) captures the variety of goods for sale and the importer GDP, the demand. Distance in this model picks up all the cost of trading. The gravity model with its formulation in terms of the economic size, distance and the dummies representative of cultural

1. It may be in order to mention in this context that the gravity model describes the pattern and behaviour of trade flows, but not economic welfare as such. To analyse welfare implications, it is appropriate to use other methodologies such as the CGE (computable general equilibrium) modelling rather than gravity. This also applies to implications relating to reallocations of labour and capital across sectors as a result of trade liberalisation for which gravity is very poorly placed and alternative methodologies, such as CGE modelling, need to be considered.

and historical proximity presents bilateral trade as a function of natural parameters, that is trade as it would be in the absence of any barriers, policy or otherwise. The coefficients that the model yields are, therefore, often used to predict the trade potentials among countries. In addition, the augmentation of the model with policy and non-policy variables helps identify the costs and/or benefits of specific policy measures. Among these, quantification of trade enhancing effects of integration through PTAs (preferential trading agreements), currency unions, membership of World Trade Organization (WTO)/multilateralism has been undertaken using the gravity model. Bilateral trade pattern analysis with reference to the potential trade estimates has been considered as basis for indicating future course correction for trade policy of individual countries. The policy implications of a negative sign (untapped export potential) in the difference between effective and potential export/potential trade go from the necessity of country-specific export promotion and of broader bilateral integration, to the need to anticipate relevant welfare implications due to the effect of the expansion in bilateral trade flows in the near future. A positive sign (successful partnership) in the difference between the effective and potential trade generates different policy implications such as trade has reached its potential level and no social cost has to be expected from future integration (Batra, 2004). The characteristics of a country's trading partners affect how much it will gain from trade. For instance, trade links with growing and technologically sophisticated markets can boost domestic productivity growth. Similarly it matters to know who the home country's 'natural trading partners' are, as this would typically depend on geography (distance, terrain), cultural and historical ties.

Quantification of export potentials is done using either of the following two estimation procedures. The first, out-of-sample export potential estimation in which case the parameters for a country and its trading partners are estimated by a gravity model and then the same coefficients are applied to project the natural trade between India and other countries. The difference between the thus predicted and observed trade flows represents the unexploited export potential. The second approach derives in-sample export potential estimates, i.e., all the trading partners are included in the regression analysis and the residuals of the estimated equation represent the difference between potential and actual trade relations.

3.2.1 Econometric Methodology

While theoretical basis to the gravity is now rich, there continues to be constant development in the literature on the subject, particularly with regard to the econometric methodology for estimation, particularly as the gravity model in an augmented form using relevant policy variables is increasingly aimed at analysing a varied set of objectives and policy questions. These aspects make it imperative that the model specification in each research application be a careful exercise updated with the latest developments in the field.

3.2.1.1 Multilateral Resistance Factor

More recent literature on gravity models following Anderson and Wincoop (2003) has accepted that bilateral trade in addition to being influenced by distance and mass, also depends on country specific trade resistance, e.g., if a country has policies or institutions that are inimical to trade its bilateral trade would be smaller or if it offered preferential access to one trade partner it could impact trade with all its partners. This is referred to as the multilateral resistance factor. Baldwin and Taglioni (2006) show that multilateral resistance terms change over time so that the use of these as identified by Anderson and Wincoop would be restricted to cross section analysis only. This has been translated in terms of including country fixed effects in cross section model estimations and failure to do so results in what Baldwin and Taglioni call the gold medal mistake. An example cited by the authors in this context is the currency union trade effect reported in Rose (2000) that gets reduced on correcting for the gold-medal mistake when pair fixed effects are used on the original data set in Rose (2001).[2] The authors then go on to identify the silver medal mistake in case the gravity model is estimated with log of

2. For more details on Rose (2000; 2001). Refer to page 81 and 82.

the average trade rather than average of the logs of trade. In case the trade between countries is balanced the error on account of this mistake would be small, but if trade is unbalanced the error would be large. The nation-specific variation for the Rose effect as evident in Micco *et al.* (2003), it is considered, is due to varying severity of the silver medal mistake. A final mistake in estimation that Baldwin and Taglioni point out is the bronze medal mistake wherein inappropriate deflation of all bilateral trade flows is undertaken with the same price index, typically the US aggregate price index. This can create spurious correlation if there are global inflationary trends in the data that affect both the left and right hand side of the gravity equation. Gravity is an expenditure function allocating nominal GDP into nominal imports; therefore inappropriate deflation probably creates biases via spurious correlations. It may however be noted that time dummies or country effects can correct for this. So that if the gold medal mistake is taken care of, the bronze would be resolved too.

3.2.1.2 Use of Panel Data

As trade liberalisation and reforms at the national, regional and multilateral levels continue, trade relationships are liable to change over time and so keeping in mind this development there is an increasing use of panel (longitudinal) data approaches to the estimation of gravity models. The use of different panel data methods, such as random or fixed (within) effects estimators, allows for various assumptions regarding trade flows to be analysed and tested. The use of panel data (over time bilateral trade data) also has the advantage of mitigating the bias generated by heterogeneity across countries. While in a single cross section, country-pair propensity to trade can only be controlled for by observed country-pair characteristics (such as common language, common currency), in a panel country-pair heterogeneity can be controlled for by using country-pair fixed effects. In many applications country heterogeneity is ignored by using (repeated) cross-section analyses, pooled OLS specifications or data averaged over longer horizons. However, ignoring country heterogeneity can lead to highly distorted estimates. In this context, Mátyás (1997; 1998) proposed to include two sets of country dummies (for exporting and importing countries). This approach was also employed by Abraham and Hove (2005) in a gravity model application to Asian countries and China. Egger and Pfaffermayr (2003) showed, however, that instead of having one dummy variable per country, individual country-pair dummies (fixed effects) and time dummies to control for common shocks should be used to get efficient estimators. Furthermore, Micco *et al.* (2003) suggest that the inclusion of country-pair fixed effects may mitigate endogeneity problems. For instance, unusually high trade flows may lead to the establishment of a FTA rather than vice versa. Country-pair fixed effects take into account whether two countries have traditionally traded a lot.

While panel data has advantages in terms of being able to capture the relevant relationships over time and panels monitor unobservable trading-partner-pairs' individual effects, classical gravity models have used cross-section data to estimate trade effects and trade relationship for a particular time period, which is invariably one particular year. Further, it has also been observed that aggregation over time does not really add any significant value to the estimations. The classical tradition of estimation with cross-section data continues to be used in the estimation of gravity model.

3.2.2 Inclusion of Policy Variables: Non-Tariff Measures (NTMs) and Trade Barriers

NTMs may be intrinsically protectionist but they may also address market failures such as externalities and information asymmetries between consumers and producers. NTMs which address market failures may restrict trade while at the same time improving welfare. Other NTMs such as certain standards or export subsidies may expand trade. NTMs are important to study because they can be distortionary in their impact on trade, even when applicable to all countries indiscriminately and whether implemented with protectionist intent or otherwise. Standards and technical requirements while being uniformly specified for all trading partner countries may be a greater barrier for low income or even developing countries that may not have the necessary resources or technology to adhere to these standards. NTMs like anti-dumping and safeguards are sometimes used as threat measures. Moreover as tariffs are being unilaterally reduced by almost all countries, there is a fear as also a tendency to develop substitute barriers and incorporate these in sophisticated policy measures to protect domestic industry. The qualification of NTMs as NTBs (non-tariff barriers) however can only be done as a result of analysis based on comprehensive data. The impact of NTM is seen in terms of cost/price enhancing effect or a trade restricting effect at the border. In both interpretations, the NTB implies a protectionist or a trade-cost effect. Essentially theoretical rationale in the context of NTMs, whether they be protectionist or aimed at other administrative or social objectives, is in terms of a shift of the supply or demand curve.

South Asian economies including India in addition to the standard NTMs have been unique in terms of the nature of NTMs devised to act as barriers to trade. Denial of MFN (most favoured nation) status by Pakistan to India has acted as a major barrier to exploiting potential trade between the two countries. India-Pakistan actual trade today is several times lower than what the two neighbouring countries could have traded in the absence of this barrier. In addition, traditional NTMs are also erected and implemented by all countries in the context of bilateral trade within the region.

Country specific NTBs in bilateral trade are cited as follows. Nepal lists problems of SPS (sanitary and phytosanitary) requirements, complex quarantine rules on agricultural products and uneven implementation of trade treaty measures by state governments in India in addition to disagreement on customs clearance procedures for cross border rail operations and CVDs (countervailing duties) as major NTBs imposed by India on its goods. Bangladesh for all seven countries and especially for India specifies lab testing of food items, chemical testing, packaging requirements, SPS, PSI (pre-shipment inspection) certification, product standards and CVDs as NTBs. Bangladesh Bank Letters of Credit rules and more generally the credibility of the Bangladesh banks have been reported to constrain Indian exports to Bangladesh, and as one of the factors responsible for illegal practices in the border trade, especially at the Petrapole-Benapole border crossing. An important general non-tariff constraint on Bangladesh's imports from India is the fact that only 4 out of the 42 customs posts on the land border with India are allowed to clear all imported goods—the others are limited to dealing with very short list of products and must obtain case by case authorisation from the National Board of Revenue for clearing anything not on the list. Additionally, apparently in a bid to restrict illegal imports, since July 2002, Bangladesh has required that two of its principal imports from India—textile yarn and sugar—can only be imported through its sea ports. Both Bangladesh and India have periodically constrained imports of certain products by specifying the ports at which they can be cleared by customs. In June 2005, India restricted the ports which can administer its various export incentive schemes. Many of the alternative ports are prohibitively costly for the northeast and eastern states in India effectively implying a ban on exports from these states to nearby regions in Bangladesh and providing an incentive to send these goods illegally. Pakistan considers PSI (pre shipment inspection) as the main obstacle in exporting to Bangladesh and refusal of letters of credit when it exports to India. In addition, Pakistan exporters have also reported sampling, customs inspection, TBTs and SPS as other NTBs in the region (Iqbal, 2012).

India imposes anti-dumping measures as a price control measure to protecting domestic production. India also insists on prior authorisation for sensitive product categories specially focusing on the GM (genetically modified) food category. Citing damage to the environment or wildlife and human life, India has placed restrictions on certain animal products, fresh fruits and vegetable coated with edible and non-edible wax. The goods that enter India are required to fulfil the marking and labelling requirements of the country. India is in the process of identifying the barriers and removing them as far as possible. Recently the Government of India has taken a decision to waive the stipulation for testing and certification of products by Indian laboratories as a precondition for imports. Instead of testing and certification by the Indian entities, it would now be enough if the job was done by laboratories in the SAARC (South Asian Association for Regional Cooperation) countries accredited by the Bureau of Indian Standards (BIS).

Recent econometric approaches to estimating NTM effects are either price-based or quantity-based. Price-based methods examine international price differences and assess the extent to which NTMs cause certain domestic prices to be higher than they would be in their absence. Quantity-based methods, by contrast, are gravity based most of the time, i.e., they use some form of the gravity model. The decision to use a price- or quantity-based method is often based on the availability of data. As data on trade flows are abundant even at a highly disaggregated level, while price data are more problematic, quantity analysis is often preferred to price analysis.

As regards the gravity model, as discussed already, while economic theory explains the complex bilateral trade patterns among countries, in the real world actual trade is much lower than the trade predicted by the model in a frictionless world. The gap between potential and actual trade has been the subject of many studies and many theories have been proposed to explain why actual bilateral trade is not as much as predicted by economic models. The deviation of actual bilateral trade from the frictionless prediction of trade allows inference about bilateral trade costs that are far larger and diverse than the transport and policy costs. One of the most compelling arguments in this context has been given by Obstfeld and Rogoff (2000) who suggested that large unobserved trade costs may be responsible for the discrepancy between projected trade figures by theoretical/empirical models/estimation and trade statistics. Anderson and Wincoop (2004) in their research indicated that the costs of trade between even the well integrated economies are more than that accounted by geographical distance and traditional trade policies. Analysis and quantification of hidden costs, thus, while having been attempted by many studies (Maskus *et al.*, 2005; Djankov *et al.*, 2010; Hoekman and Nicita, 2011) are constrained by data. Data on trading costs are mostly available with respect to tariff costs and very few databases[3] provide information on NTBs and behind the border barriers and costs of trading among nations.

---

3. These include Doing Business database, Logistics Performance Index, Trade Facilitation Database, and the UNCTAD Trade Analysis and Information System (TRAINS).

The gravity model has been used to measure the impact of NTMs. In empirical estimation of measuring the NTM impact most gravity models use dummy variables, AVEs (ad valorem equivalent measures) of the policies, frequency ratios and count variables. The disaggregated product level with a restricted country set has often been the chosen estimation framework for NTM analysis. A disaggregated representation of the NTM, generally possible for a technical measure, helps separate identification of supply and demand effects. However, it needs to be recognised that the gravity model has originally been formulated and estimated with trade at the aggregate level as the dependent variable and extending the logic of the gravity equation to sectoral trade flows (trade in one particular good) is not entirely straightforward. In the monopolistic-competition model, larger countries produce more varieties of goods and that contributes to increasing their trade. That is, they do not necessarily trade more of each good but they trade more goods. Thus, the idea that trade flows between two countries is increasing in a certain sector owing to the increase in one's GDP is not necessarily warranted. In Batra (2013), conflict, which has been and continues to be the biggest challenge and barrier to exploitation of trade potential in South Asia, has been used as an explanatory variable in the gravity model. The formulation of the gravity model explains causality of bilateral trade in terms of conflict. Trade costs of bilateral and regional conflict are then estimated. As conflict is a country-level barrier it is only appropriate to consider aggregate trade as in the classical tradition as the dependent variable.

Trade barriers though may be, in some cases, of particular relevance at the sector level. In such instances aggregation of trade barriers into an overall index filters out a lot of useful information, which explains their usual absence from aggregate gravity equations (trade barriers being bunched with country fixed effects or in the error term). However, when analysing sectoral trade flows, aggregation is no longer a pretext there and so trade barriers ought to be included explicitly in the equation. Indeed, at the sectoral level the gravity equation becomes a good vehicle for analysing how sector specific trade barriers affect trade flows. This may also be justified based on the recent empirical research (e.g. Hummels and Klenow, 2005) suggesting that trade expands both at the extensive margin (more products) and at the intensive one (more volume for each product) as economies grow, even though there would be the risk of finding an insignificant coefficient on exporter GDP.

3.2.3 Gravity Model and Trade Agreements

In theoretical discussions, outcomes of multilateral negotiations are considered to be 'first-best' solutions to trade policy issues. RTAs (regional trade agreements), given that they are by definition preferential and hence discriminatory, can in comparison provide only second best solutions. However, there is another side to the argument that proposes that ever expanding RTAs would eventually bring the world closer to the desired objective of free trade through multilateralism. Also, regionalism and PTAs (preferential trade agreements) have become the preferred mode of trade liberalisation among countries given the slow progress of the Doha round at the Wrld Trade Organization (WTO). It is considered that the regional/bilateral FTAs (free trade agreements) can be advantageous to the participant countries as they can negotiate aspects of trade that are either too difficult or not on the agenda under the Doha Development Agenda (DDA) at the WTO. The bilateral agreements can thus provide alternative means to economic gains for countries that have similar interests. There is increasingly an attempt by most countries to design the bilateral agreements towards deeper integration objectives even if selectively so. Even the relative latecomers in this process have evolved their FTAs to maximise the potential benefits from these agreements.

The literature on RTAs is focused on two variables, viz., welfare effects and trade flows. Gravity models have been used to measure the effects of RTAs and the impact of unobserved trade barriers on trade flows. Regional integration initiatives such as FTAs, customs unions and especially the monetary unions have been analysed for their impact on regional trade using the gravity model. Tinbergen (1962) was the first to provide an econometric study using a gravity equation for international trade flows, and the first estimates of the effects of FTAs on trade flows. His results were mixed as he found the membership of the British Commonwealth to result in significantly higher trade flows while that of the Benelux FTA did not lead to a significant impact on trade flows. Given the accelerated pace at which countries around the world are entering into preferential trading arrangements in the 1990s, many studies have been undertaken to estimate the impact of these arrangements on bilateral trade flows using the gravity model. Frankel and Wei (1997) have examined the effects of membership in seven trade blocs like the EFTA (European Free Trade Association), EC (now EU), NAFTA (North American Free Trade Agreement), Mercosur and the Andean group, ASEAN and the Australia-New Zealand (ANZ) Closer economic relations agreement on trade flows. EC, Mercosur, ANZ and ASEAN countries show a significant intra-regional trade bias. Soloaga and Winters (1999) have used a modified gravity model to identify the separate effects of PTAs on intra bloc trade, members' total imports, and members' total exports. A pre and post membership analysis is also undertaken in their study. Their estimates do not give any indication of the new wave of regionalism having significantly boosted intra bloc trade flows. They find convincing evidence of trade diversion only for EU and EFTA. For the same blocs export diversion was also observed. In all these studies a membership dummy variable has been used to examine the trade effects of an FTA. The estimation was more detailed in later analysis by Baier and Bergstrand (2002) and Carrere (2003), where panel data estimation was undertaken, revealing larger impact of the FTAs.

With a panel data set that includes bilateral observations for five years spanning 1970 through 1990 for 186 countries Rose (2000) highlights the common currency impact of a currency union on trade using a gravity model in its augmented form with two additional variables for currency union and volatility of bilateral nominal exchange rate in the period. While Currency Union membership is indicated through a binary dummy variable in the data set, the standard deviation of the first-difference of the monthly natural logarithm of the bilateral nominal exchange rate in the five years preceding period is used to measure the volatility of the exchange rate. Results of separate regressions for the five years of the sample as also a pooled regression (with year controls) are reported by the author. The estimates show that trade is substantially higher for countries that use the same currency, holding other things equal. Countries with volatile exchange rates also trade less. Both effects are significant at conventional statistical levels. Several sensitivity tests are carried out with alternative specifications of exchange rate volatility, stricter definitions of a currency union and alternative estimation methods are undertaken to ensure robustness of the results.[4]

To address the effect of an FTA on the direction of trade, initially the basic gravity model was extended with the inclusion of one single regional dummy to capture the effect of the FTA on intra-regional trade; another set of dummies was included in later works to capture the FTA's trade diversion effects on non-members (Soloaga and Winters 2001). Trade diversion has been estimated by some studies by adding a non-FTA member dummy to the standard estimable equation. The dummy takes the value of unity if one country belongs to an FTA but the other country does not, to capture trade diversion effect. Urata and Okabe (2007) in their paper estimate the trade diversion effects in this manner and for a more precise assessment of the impact of FTAs, the FTA and non-FTA dummies in their sample are given the value of unity when FTAs in question are in effect and an FTA country pair dummy variable is introduced, which takes the value of unity for the entire sample period regardless of the status of FTAs. Such treatment would enable to isolate the impact of FTAs.

3.2.4 Gravity Model and Services Trade

Notwithstanding data limitations, some studies have used the gravity model to identify determinants of services trade while others have examined the possibility of extending the applicability of the gravity model to services trade. Country specific focus, particularly for India has not been the mainstay of these studies. Grünfeld and

4. Rose (2001) provides a correction for the size of the currency union effect. This has been discussed in the context of the gold medal mistake in a gravity model. Refer to page 75.

Moxnes (2003), Kimura (2003), Kimura and Lee (2004), Mirza and Nicoletti (2004) were among the first studies to use the OECD data set on bilateral trade in services in a gravity framework to analyse the determinants of bilateral services trade. Walsh (2006) also uses the OECD data set but with five disaggregated service categories of total services, government services, transport, travel and other commercial services as dependent variables. As regards the impact of FTAs on services trade, while the Grünfeld and Moxnes analysis finds trade agreements to be insignificant in determining services trade, Kimura and Lee find a positive impact of the FTAs. In the Indian context, inclusion of services sector liberalisation is evident only in the comprehensive trade agreements that India has with Japan, South Korea and Singapore and only partially in case of the India-Malaysia CEPA (Comprehensive Economic Partnership Agreement). Analysis of possible implications towards enhancing trade potential or altered trade patterns specifically for the services sector is not evident in the available literature.

Shingal (2009) uses the gravity model to distil the trade effects of RTAs into those emanating from services and 'only goods' RTAs and also disaggregates the relationship between RTAs and bilateral services trade according to the economic status of the partner countries. For RTAs that are 'only goods' in nature, incremental impact of services has been examined by the author. The fact that all trading partners that have a services RTA also have a goods FTA and that there are some trade partners in the sample that have only a goods RTA enables the isolation of a 'goods only' RTA and a 'pseudo-incremental' impact of a services agreement. Though the analysis is not undertaken with an Indian perspective, it is useful to highlight the findings given the comprehensive nature of India's new trade agreements. The gravity model is estimated in a log-linear form, setting bilateral services trade data in a panel, available from the OECD's database for 25 exporting and 53 importing countries for five years over 1999-2003. The estimation results suggest a trade effect of 11.6 per cent from having a services RTA alone. This effect rises to 12.7 per cent for the non-EU trading partners in the sample. The incremental impact of an "only goods" RTA in addition to a services RTA is found to be 2.3 to 2.4 per cent for this set of countries. North-South services agreements are found to be, by and large, more conducive to raising bilateral services exports between trading partners compared to any RTA or goods-only agreements and this trade effect emanates largely from asymmetric nature of North-South agreements.

3.3 Gravity Model: Empirical Evidence

3.3.1 India's Trade Potential

The gravity model has been used in an augmented form by Batra (2004) to first analyse India's bilateral trade flows with its trade partners and then estimate its global trade potential. The model is augmented in that the estimable equation includes, other than income and distance, several other variables that may have an impact on bilateral trade. The set of additional variables represent proximity for a bilateral pair of countries in terms of history, culture, geography, all variables that would in an ideal world enhance the trade potential for any country.

$$\text{Log}(T_{ij}) = \alpha + \beta_1 \log(Y_i Y_j) + \beta_2 \log(Y_i/pop_i . Y_j/pop_j) + \beta_3 \log(D_{ij}) + \beta_4 (Border_{ij}) + \beta_5 (Lang_{ij}) + \gamma 1(Regl) + \gamma 2(Comcol) + \gamma 3(Col) + \gamma 4 (landlocked) + \gamma 5 (Island) + u_{ij} \ldots\ldots\ldots (3)$$

Where

i and j denote countries.

T_{ij} denotes the value of bilateral trade between i and j.

D_{ij} is bilateral distance.

The following proximity variables are included represented by binary dummies:

$Border_{ij}$: shared/common borders between the countries in the trading pair

$Lang_{ij}$: common language.

Comcol: common coloniser.

The estimable equation also includes dummy variables that assume a value of 0/1/2 depending on the number of countries in a trading pair that have the following geographical characteristics:

Landlocked: Number of landlocked countries in the trading pair.

Island: Number of island countries in the trading pair.

Analysing the bilateral trade patterns the estimated equation for gravity model in Batra (2004) also looks at the impact, if any, of the PTAs that the countries in a trading pair may be in the reference period.

Regl: Regional trading arrangement.

The model is estimated using nominal GNP (gross national product) in terms of US dollars as well as GNP in PPP (purchasing power parity) terms. While it is generally considered that GNPppp has no bearing on trade as it usually happens in international prices, the estimation with GNPppp helps account for the strong undervaluation of GNP for some countries, importantly for India. The estimation also includes GNP per capita as an independent variable in an attempt to explore the link between a country's trade and its stage of development. Innovation processes that would feed into export demand may be a function of the level of development. Further, GNP per capita is also considered as the critical variable that would help ascertain the relevance of either the Helpman-Krugman kind of hypothesis that predicts that trade should increase with increasingly equal distribution of income or the H-O trade theories that says that countries with dissimilar levels of income will trade more than those with similar levels of income. In addition, the coefficient of the GNP per capita variable provides insight in terms of the Linder hypothesis according to which trade is more among countries with similar levels of income as even they are likely to have similar preferences and similar but differentiated products. In order to distinguish between the influences of the H-O style factor endowment differences, Linder style differences in taste and the effect of development on trade as also to capture the distinctive features of each, the gravity model as estimated by Batra (2004) includes a term for the difference in per capita GNP.

The model is estimated using the OLS methodology, cross-section data for the year 2000 with bilateral merchandise trade as the dependent variable. The data set covers 146 countries with partners drawn form a set of 245 countries. Overall the sample is representative of about 90 per cent of world trade. The data for bilateral trade is derived from the UNCOMTRADE. World Development Indicators (WDI) of the World Bank are used for variables like the GDP and population while the CEPII is used for distance and other standard gravity model control variables.[5] All estimates are checked for heteroscedasticity. The coefficients thus obtained are in the second stage used to estimate the potential trade for India at the global level. The analysis is undertaken at a detailed level to analyse India's trading pattern and some regional trading arrangements. In particular SAARC, ASEAN and GCC (Gulf Cooperation Council) are analysed. India's trade relationship with China is also taken up for analysis. The estimation takes care of econometric issues of multicolleanrity and endogeneity testing for correlations and Klein's thumb rule for the former and using instrumental variables in case of the latter. Pairs of countries with zero trade value have been dealt with by undertaking estimation with alternative methodologies like omission of the country pairs with zero trade, estimation of a restricted model for only those countries that have income above US $15 million and lastly by using a semi-log formulation of the gravity model that is then estimated using the Tobit model. The results do not alter significantly across these variations in estimation. The results are robust.

The first stage results show the standard gravity model variables to be correctly signed and statistically significant. GNP, distance and common border appear as significant variables with GNP and common border impacting positively and significantly on bilateral trade and distance having a negative and significant impact. In the model two countries that share a common border are estimated to engage in 75 per cent more trade relative to two otherwise similar countries. Other variables of proximity also have positive implications for bilateral trade. Cultural proximity represented by linguistic similarity that is a common language increases bilateral trade by 74 per cent while, historical proximity as evident in ex-colonies and common colonisers makes bilateral trade disproportionately intense. Variables representing geographical limitations like landlockedness expectedly

5. *www.cepii.fr.*

imply reduction in trade (by 30%) owing to lack of ocean ports. When the estimation is undertaken for GNPppp, the variables do not show any significant change. The results also indicate that trade and development relationship is the most significant channel through which per capita income is likely to impact trade. Following these results, Batra (2004) undertakes to estimate India's trade potential with its partner countries. The potential trade so estimated is then compared with actual levels of trade with these partner countries. The countries where the potential has been fulfilled and where there is large gap between the potential and actual are identified. The latter group of countries are classified as countries with scope for expansion of trade with India.

Interestingly, the possibility of expanding trade is highest with countries like China, United Kingdom, Pakistan, Japan, Italy, and France. The estimates indicate the potential to be 10 times higher than the actual level of trade for countries like Georgia, Turkmenistan, and Uzbekistan. Countries with which trade ought to be 5 times or more than the actual trade include Lithuania, Tajikistan, Mongolia, Romania, Luxembourg, and Norway. Potential trade, that is more than twice the level of actual trade, is indicated for countries like China, Japan, Austria, Mexico, Qatar etc. Region-wise maximum potential is indicated for the Asia-Pacific region followed by Western Europe, North America, Middle East, Central and Eastern Europe, and Latin America. In Asia, Japan, Pakistan, China, Philippines, and Korea reveal maximum potential for expansion of trade with India. Among the set of countries comprising the EU, India has trade potential with all except Belgium. In North America, both the US and Canada reveal considerable potential for expanding trade. In Central and Eastern Europe, Poland, has the maximum potential for expansion of trade with India. For the Commonwealth of Independent States (CIS), the estimates indicate India's trade with the region as a whole as also with member countries like Russia, Ukraine, and Belarus has exceeded the potential.

As regards regional groupings India's trade potential is examined for SAARC, ASEAN and GCC. In case of SAARC, not surprisingly, the maximum trade potential, well beyond the actual levels, is indicated with Pakistan. For ASEAN, high trade potential is indicated for Philippines, Vietnam and Cambodia. With Thailand trade potential is predicted only when estimates are undertaken with GNP in PPP terms. Countries in ASEAN with which India's trade is in excess of potential include Singapore, Malaysia, and Indonesia. Among the countries of the GCC, potential is indicated with Oman, Kuwait, and Qatar. Trade is predicted to be thrice and twice its actual level in case of Oman and Qatar respectively. India has the highest trade with UAE followed by Saudi Arabia in the GCC (Table 3.1).

Table 3.1

India's Trade Potential

GCC			ASEAN			SAARC		
Country	P/A_{ppp}	P/A_C	*Country*	P/A_{PPP}	P/A_C	*Country*	P/A_{PPP}	P/A_C
Oman	4.4	3	Cambodia	7.9	3.3	Pakistan	52.2	26.7
Qatar	—	2	Philippines	5.5	2.3	Nepal	1.3	0.8
Kuwait	2.1	1.6	Vietnam	2	1	Maldives	1	0.7
Bahrain	1.3	0.9	Thailand	1.9	1	Sri Lanka	1	0.5
Saudi Arabia	1.1	0.8	Indonesia	0.8	0.4	Bangladesh	—	—
UAE	—	—	Malaysia	0.5	0.3	Bhutan	—	—
			Singapore	0.5	0.3			
			Laos	—	—			
			Myanmar	—	—			
			Brunei	—	—			

Notes: P: potential trade; A: actual trade, c: current international.

Source: Batra, 2004.

Outside of regions and regional groupings, the India-China bilateral trade stands out as having a vast potential for expansion. The gravity model yields a value that is 2.5 times the actual trade in 2000 as potential for trade between India and China. The common membership of PTAs like the APTA (Asia Pacific Trade Agreement) further enhances this potential.

Tharakan *et al.* (2005) apply the gravity model specification to evaluate the differential determinants of India's bilateral software and total goods exports. They implement a restricted gravity model which deals with the exports of software of one country (India) to all the other countries, and not the bilateral trade between all countries of the world. In addition to bilateral distance, a remoteness variable defined as the average weighted distance of the partner country from all its other potential trading partners is included in the estimable equation. The authors expect a significant coefficient for both distance and remoteness variables in case of services exports if information asymmetries, as proxied by distance, matter. For total goods exports the distance variable, they expect, should yield the traditional negative sign, whereas the remoteness term is expected to yield a positive and significant result. An interesting additional variable to represent i.e., People of Indian Origin (PIO, as a proportion of total partner country population) who, according to the authors, could be facilitating software exports is also added to the estimable equation. Using Tobit model for the period of 1997-2001, they find distance to be insignificant in comparing Indian software exports to overall goods trade flows, implying thereby that distance is not an important trade resistance factor in India's software exports. The English language dummy has a positive impact on software exports but no significance for other exports. Network connections as represented by PIO turn out to be significant for both goods and software exports. Robustness checks are undertaken with alternative fixed effects model with no major changes in the results.

Bhattacharyya and Banerjee (2006) apply the gravity model to a set of countries with which India had trade relations at least once between 1950 and 2000 in a cross section and panel data estimation. They find that India's trade responds less than proportionally to size and more than proportionally to distance. The analysis however does not take into account the fundamental differences in orientation of the Indian economic policy towards trade and external sector over the long reference period. A sub-period analysis may have been more worthwhile in providing useful insights on trade patterns. Using gravity model, Bhattacharya's (2004) paper undertakes a comparative analysis and simulates the increase in India-Bangladesh bilateral trade under four hypothetical scenarios of differing tariff rate cuts.

The author finds that in free trade regime India's exports will be more than the increase in its imports from Bangladesh.

Tripathi and Leitao (2013) apply the gravity model for a restricted set of 'major' trade partners for India. Using a panel data set they estimate a gravity model for India's trade with China PRP, United Arab Emirates, United States, Saudi Arab, Switzerland, Singapore, Germany, Hong Kong, Indonesia, Iraq, Japan, Belgium, Kuwait, Korea RP, Nigeria, Australia, United Kingdom, Iran, South Africa, and Qatar for the period 1998-2012. Applying Tobit, random effects and GMM (generalised method of moments) estimator analysis they arrive at much the same conclusions for all the standard variables used by most earlier studies. They provide an additional variable of political proximity in terms of number of trade partners' embassies located in India and the results show it to have a positive impact on trade. The only variable that they find giving a contrarion result is distance, which in their study is revealed to have a positive coefficient instead of the expected negative sign, even though the statistical significance of the variable is not very high. The authors while noting this variation in their result, in terms of intuition, theory and prior studies provide no explanation to this effect. De (2010) estimates a standard gravity model to analyze India's trade flows and also makes an attempt to assess the impact of tariff and transaction costs on India's exports with a limited set of 'major' trade partners for the period 1995-2007. The analysis reiterates the huge gap between India's potential and actual trade with Pakistan. The results also show, as expected, tariff and transaction costs to be negatively related to trade flows. The paper makes a projection for potential trade based on IMF GDP projections for 2014. However given the uncertainties engendered in the global economy by the global financial crisis and the consequent quarterly changes in projections by official agencies as also national government agencies, the projected post global financial crisis trade potential may not be accurately reflective of the actual potential.

3.3.2. India's FTAs: Bilateral, Regional and Extra-Regional

India has been a latecomer to the process of regionalism as reflected in the pursuit of FTAs. While it has had a long standing tradition of trade treaties with its smaller neighbours like Bhutan and Nepal, these have not been in the nature of WTO defined FTA formulation. Notwithstanding, the trade treaties have created a de facto free trade area between India and Nepal, and India and Bhutan. So while being traditionally loyal to multilateralism, India started to pursue formal bilateral FTAs in the 2000s and now both strategies are simultaneously pursued by the Indian policymakers. Within South Asia, India's first and only FTA agreement with Sri Lanka was implemented in 2000. Outside South Asia, India entered into a comprehensive economic partnership with Singapore in 2005 and more recently in 2009, signed the trade agreement with ASEAN and South Korea and with Japan in 2010. As most of these FTAs have been focused only on trade in goods, they aim at 'shallow integration'. Given that India's growth process is led by the services sector, the limited coverage of the FTAs has led to some scepticism in terms of their beneficial impact.

India's more recent new age trade agreements that are more comprehensive in coverage may have greater potential for efficient trade creation as they are formulated with more liberal provisions. The comprehensive economic partnerships and cooperation agreements have included provisions with regard to selective liberalisation of the services as well as investment sectors. The India-Korea FTA liberalises 75 per cent of India's tariff lines within eight years and 93 per cent of South Korea's tariff lines (Wignaraja, 2011). The India-Korea CEPA was signed in 2009 after a three-year period of negotiations, with inclusion of provisions for deeper integration through goods, investment and services liberalisation. The CEPA, which has been in effect since January 2010, has a symbolic importance in being the first between a major industrial powerhouse and a BRIC (association of the emerging economies of Brazil, Russia, India and China) economy. The agreement, by undertaking to eliminate tariffs on 85 to 90 per cent of mutually traded goods, aims to double bilateral trade from its 2008 level of US$15.6 billion. Through this deal, India has also been able to secure an opening for the liberalisation of its services sector with a major economy and in sectors/areas where it has comparative advantage, that is, the ICT sector and temporary movement to Korea of service professionals. India has also agreed to provide better investor protection to induce increased investment flow from Korea. The India-Japan EPA (economic partnership agreement), negotiations for which began in 2007 and was signed in 2010, is likely to provide major benefits to the dwindling Japanese economy by tariff cuts on offer in the auto parts sector. Japan has offered to cut tariffs on farm products and Indian tea. In addition, it is also to provide for the movement of professionals in the health sector, while facilitating Japanese investment into India. The trade pact is thus envisioned to benefit both countries. Services liberalisation to a limited extent is thus seen in India's FTA with Singapore and Korea and Japan. Three Singapore issues have been included in the India-South Korea FTA. On Government procurement, even though there is no separate chapter, there is cooperation provision on procurement thus making possible liberalisation in this difficult area.

Plummer (2007) defines the 'best practices' for FTAs such that they approximate 'first best solution' to the greatest extent possible in practical terms. On the basis of what is called the 10 commandments of regionalism Plummer makes an assessment of the Asian FTAs. In the Plummer taxonomy India-Singapore is a 'full' FTA that included provisions towards liberalisation of goods, services and investment. Product specific and general RoO (rules of origin), FDI, negative list for services, movement of professional were all specified in the text of the bilateral comprehensive agreement. Further, as graded by Plummer(2007) based upon WTO compliance and outward orientation, the only FTA/CEPA that attains only a B or C grade with respect to the goods and services liberalisation is the India and Singapore CECA (comprehensive economic cooperation agreement).[6]

As a member of the SAARC, India has been a signatory to the South Asian Free Trade Area (SAFTA) agreement that was signed in 2006. Prior to SAFTA, India initiated the FTA process in South Asia through its bilateral agreement with Sri Lanka. SAFTA was however criticised (Batra, 2005) after its formulation and implementation

6. The India-Korea and India-Japan comprehensive agreements that have been signed more recently may also be similarly classified given that these are India's first attempts at 'deeper' economic integration.

in 2006 for having excluded the potentially more beneficial services sectors for liberalisation and preferential access. The agreement towards services liberalisation for South Asian countries has been negotiated, finalised and signed separately from SAFTA only in 2010, while that for investment liberalisation, even though finalised is yet to be signed. Further, the coverage of goods for preferential access under SAFTA has been limited and Pakistan has for long acted in contravention of the agreement by specifying a positive list as opposed to the agreed upon procedure of a negative list specification. SAFTA has not been able to provide any significant momentum to intra-regional trade in South Asia that continues to hover around 4-5 per cent of the member countries total trade. Appropriately, therefore, in the Plummer (2007) taxonomy, SAFTA is classified as a limited FTA. As further identified by Plummer, the positive list approach to the creation of the FTAs is possibly the worst possible approach as it tends to increase the scope for trade diversion and reduce the scope for trade creation. In South Asia, SAPTA the precursor to SAFTA was based on a positive list approach. Even the products that were included in the positive list and the concessions that were granted were restricted to only a few sectors like chemicals, textiles and clothing and machinery and appliances and some in the category of live animals and animal products. It has been estimated that the proportion of intra-regional imports covered by SAPTA preferences was highest for Pakistan (39.6%), followed by Nepal (35.2%), India (30%), Bhutan (17%) and Sri Lanka (12%). The import value coverage for Bangladesh and Maldives was marginal (Mukherjee, 2004). While the SAFTA made a correction by adopting the negative list approach, Pakistan's positive list approach and the overwhelming factor of 'conflict' ensured that the most traded commodities were excluded from preferential access (Batra, 2013). The initial negative list comprising over 50 per cent of exportable items was large. Later, in a move to enhance intra-regional trade potential of the Agreement it was decided that all SAFTA signatories will reduce their negative list by 20 per cent of tariff lines and the commodities thus excluded were to be accorded preferential treatment from January 2012 with a specified phase out period. As per the revised list, India has the least number of products on its negative list for LDCs (least developed countries) (384) and for non-LDCs (NLDCs) the 695 items are next only to Maldives specification of 545 products. Nepal has the longest list with 1,036 items, followed by Bangladesh (993), Pakistan (936) and Sri Lanka (834). Bhutan has been an exception in this regard, which will consider requests, if any, from member countries. The phase out period for tariff reduction (0-5%) is three years for NLDC to NLDCs, six years for Sri Lanka, eight years for LDCs to all contracting states and three years for NLDCs to LDCs. Pakistan continued with the positive list approach vis a vis India. This was in contradiction of the provisions of the SAFTA agreement. Pakistan has only recently, in 2011, as part of a trade normalisation process with India, notified a negative list of 1,209 items. Again as per Plummers taxonomy, the easier to liberalise services like movement of professionals, tourism, high-tech services which in case of South Asia also happen to be potentially beneficial were excluded from the initial specification of SAFTA, contributing further to its limited and inefficient design.

Among the best practices for trade creating FTAs, Plummer (2007) also specifies efficient customs practices as being at the heart of trade facilitation and as a contributory factor in designing efficient FTAs. The SAFTA provisions in Article 8 make clear the regional economies' intent to adopt practices towards facilitating trade in the region but at the same time it has been lacking in clearly stating the 'action plan' for trade facilitation in the region. The World Bank provides an evaluation of the extent of trade facilitation with regard to barriers at or behind the border such as protracted customs regulation, port fees and charges, lack of transport infrastructure and logistics services as the LPI (logistics performance index). South Asia has an average LPI score of 2.3 which is lower than the index value of 2.47 for the lower middle income group and only marginally higher than the 2.29 index value for the low income group. While India's LPI score is comparable with other low income countries, its weakest performance is in the area of customs procedures. Other South Asian countries rank lower than India in their LPI performance. Overall it would not be unfair to say that while South Asia lacks in trade logistic indicators and customs procedures are protracted and cumbersome, the regional FTA has not made any effort in terms of concrete action to facilitate trade. In terms of best practices, therefore, the regional FTA falls well short of the parameters of best practices in this respect.

The regional FTA, SAFTA, has been analysed for its trade creation impact on the member countries. The case of South Asian integration is taken up in the context of the unique and central position that India occupies in the region and that makes it and the region capable of taking forward the idea of regional economic integration in South Asia. Apart from the centrality that India enjoys in terms of geography and common borders or in terms of share in regional GDP and trade, there is the post 1991 economic dynamism that has accorded it the possible role of the lead economy in the integration process. The SAFTA analysis is therefore undertaken to not just review the efficiency aspect but also in the context of prevailing fears among the smaller economies of the region of trade gains from preferential access accruing to the larger economy, that is, India. Selective studies and their findings on distribution of trade gains among the regional economies are discussed below.

3.3.2.1 SAPTA, SAFTA and Distribution of Trade Gains to India and the Smaller Regional Economies

Earlier studies with respect to South Asian integration show this to be the only region that behaves like an exception to the natural trading blocs argument. Frankel (1997) reports that trade between the two South Asian economies India and Pakistan was 70 per cent less than two otherwise identical economies. Hirantha (2004) has used the gravity model analysis to evaluate the progress of SAPTA and the prospects for SAFTA using data from the IMF Direction of Trade Statistics for 1996-2002. Seven regional blocks and two bilateral trade agreements, identified on the basis of member countries having regular and significant trade with South Asian economies, are included in the estimation. Trade diversion has been estimated using an additional variable for trade with non-members. Results of the gravity model estimation using both panel data and cross sectional data over three time points show that there is a significant trade creation effect under SAPTA and no evidence of trade diversion effect with the rest of the world.

Coulibaly (2004) using an extended gravity model with a data set built by Rose (2003)[7] for 98 developed and developing countries, estimated the trade creation and trade diversion effects of several regional trade agreements including the impact on individual members. SAPTA along with six other trade blocs is considered for analysis. Instrumental variables are used to correct for endogeneity and measurement error problems that arise out of interpolated data for missing values of GDP and GDP per capita. In order to deal with zero trade flows, the author uses the Heckman two-step approach. Since the reference period is long, a time trend common for all country pairs is included in addition to the time fixed effects. SAPTA is found to be net export creating with potential for intra bloc export creation as well. Among member countries only Maldives and India are found to have gained through accession to the RTA. Rahman *et al.* (2006) applied an augmented gravity model to SAPTA and nine additional regional trading blocs. To capture the intra-bloc and net export effect, two separate dummy variables have been introduced in the model. Estimation is undertaken using panel data with country pair and year specific fixed effects over the reference period 1991-2003. Estimation results show a significant intra-regional trade creation and net export diversion for SAPTA. The study found that the larger economies of the region—India, Pakistan, and Bangladesh —would gain from SAPTA but the others might be adversely affected. A regional (SAARC) dummy was also found to be insignificant in the study by Rahman (2003).

The study by Rodrígueez-Delgado (2007) used a modified gravity equation to provide a quantitative evaluation of the potential impact of SAFTA with a focus on SAFTA's trade liberalisation programme with a 26 country data set for the period 1988-2004. Two versions of the gravity equation are estimated, one, in which the responsiveness of imports to changes in tariffs is allowed to vary by sources and two,

7. Andrew Rose's homepage *http://faculty.haas.berkeley.edu/arose/RecRes.htm* is an example of data sharing as his data is easily replicable.

in which case the responsiveness of imports to changes in tariffs is restricted to be the same across sources. Two sets of scenarios are then simulated with the impact of SAFTA tariff rates and the extension of SAFTA to trade agreements with other RTAs respectively with their specific TLPs (tariff liberalisation programmes). As regards, trade flows generated by SAFTA, the results show that the smallest countries like Bhutan and Maldives would gain significantly while India, Bangladesh, Pakistan, and Sri Lanka would experience increase in trade flows of a relatively smaller magnitude. In the simulations, the SAFTA TLP influences regional trade flows mainly by increasing India's exports, and imports from Bangladesh and Nepal.

Tumbarello's (2007) study that not only distinguishes between the RTA effects but also between WTO and RTA engendered trade liberalisation, suggests that during 1984-2005 membership in the RTAs in Asia, including for SAPTA does not generally appear to have led to trade diversion. Different specifications of the gravity model, with year specific effects and importer and exporter fixed effects, however show that SAPTA does not seem to have boosted intra trade flows among members to a significantly greater extent than with non-members.

ADB (2008) estimates a standard gravity model that also includes tariffs for importer and exporter countries. The model is estimated for the 7 SAARC economies in a panel data framework over the 10 year period of 1995-2005 using country pair specific and year-specific effects. The model has been estimated using annual trade data at the aggregate level and for some selected sectors as well. The fixed effects model estimation results reveal the model to perform as per *a priori* expectations. The variable representing weighted tariffs has a negative and statistically significant coefficient. The border dummy is not found to be significant and this is explained on the basis of informal trade having been the pre-dominant mode of trading rather than the formal trade. The hidden costs of trading through the formal route or the inhibiting factor on the normal route is, as is well known, prevailing conflict and consequent risks of frictions escalating to a violent event. These costs have been modelled in Batra (2013) where consequently border appears as a negative and significant variable.

The details of this study are taken up later in this paper in the context of trade costs. The estimates of potential trade in the ADB (2008) study show it to be 120 per cent more than the actual trade in 2004. But the study also avers to the fact that the gap between actual trade and potential trade may be reduced by elimination of tariffs but not fully. Eighty (80) per cent of the 120 per cent potential trade may be achieved by removal of tariffs. The rest can be attained only if other factors like NTBs and political constraints are taken care off. The gap between potential and actual trade is maximum between India and Bangladesh and India and Pakistan.

Akhter and Ghani (2010) also undertake a gravity model analysis for the SAARC economies to examine if a FTA would imply economic gains for the member economies and estimate the extent of possible trade diversion and trade creation on account of a trade agreement among these economies. The analysis is undertaken for the years 2003 to 2008, both, with cross-section data for each year and for pooled data for the entire time period. The model formulation is in the nature of a standard gravity model and is inclusive of tariffs. The model is restricted to 28 regular and significant trade partners of the South Asian countries. A generalised least square estimation is undertaken once with SAFTA as the only trading bloc and second with SAFTA and three other trading blocs, i.e., ASEAN, NAFTA and EU. For each trading block, though, only the countries that are among the 28 trading partners would be included. Other than the standard gravity model variables that are found to have the *a priori* expected sign, the coefficient of SAFTA has a negative sign indicative therefore of its potential for trade diversion. However in an interesting formulation, the authors estimate the impact of a South Asian trade agreement that is limited to India, Pakistan and Sri Lanka. This limited trade agreement has a positive potential, in that it could potentially increase trade to 30 times the existing trade levels among these countries.

Moinuddin (2013) examines the trade effects that SAPTA and SAFTA have generated since their inception using the gravity model formulation. The study is undertaken with a data set of 43 countries in accordance with their importance in South Asian trade. The analysis is focused on SAFTA and the period of reference for the study is 1992-2011. A panel data estimation is undertaken for the reference period. The model is formulated with exports as the dependent variable as it is considered that FTA analysis such as the distinction between the impacts of FTA formation on exports from a non-member to members and of exports from a FTA member to a non-member. Other than the standard variables this study includes an explanatory variable for exchange rate variation for its impact on trade flows among the sample countries. Country pair foreign exchange rates are used in the estimable equation. The estimable equation however does not include the variable for colonial links and common language as these variables are considered not directly impinging on the regional or global integration trends of the South Asian economies. A selective data set as opposed to a global data set in a way allows such liberties. Instead the variables considered more relevant to explaining South Asian economies' trade integration trends such as trade openness and restrictiveness are included for estimation. Several variations are included for the representative variables in this context. Openness of the economy has been indicated using the standard import to GDP ratio. Additionally openness is considered better represented by the ratio of total tariff revenue of the importing country to imports. The variable is expected to yield a negatively signed coefficient. Trade restrictiveness is also indicated by the applied tariff of the importing country. The variable use for this purpose is the 'OTRI' (overall trade restrictiveness index) as developed by Kee *et al.* (2009). The OTRI "reflects the uniform equivalent tariff of a country's tariff schedule and NTMs that would maintain the domestic import levels, including preferential tariffs."[8] A binary dummy variable has been included to examine the impact of MFA phase out starting 2005 at which point and after it is given a value of zero, and one for the years prior to the start of the phase out. A binary dummy is also used for membership of SAFTA. The variable is one if both countries in the trading pair are members and zero otherwise and a positive coefficient would be indicative of the trade creating potential of the regional trading

8. *http://info.worldbank.org/etools/wti/3a.asp#*

agreement. No variable for individual membership is included as the study is focused on the trade creating impact of the FTA. Zero trade values are dropped for estimation. The panel least squares estimation is undertaken for both fixed and random effects model. The results of the estimation show standard variables to behave in an expected fashion. The exchange rate variable however is revealed to have a negative sign and is low in value implying the negligible significance of exchange rate variation in export performance of the countries in the region. Trade openness shows positive links with export performance. Trade restrictiveness indices though do not have signs in accordance with *a priori* expectations. The MFA dummy is positively signed with a high value of the coefficient indicating the significant contribution that the preferential access of the quota system allowed the South Asian economies, particularly the smaller economies of the region like Bangladesh. However the paper also notes the continuing good performance of Bangladesh in the global market for apparel and garments in the post-MFA (multi-fibre arrangement) period, explained by the specialisation/expertise that the producers have acquired over a period of time and increasing labour costs in China. While these explanations could to some extent explain the continuing success of Bangladesh's exports in the global market, this may not be the entire story. After all, it is also well known that the rising costs of labour in the Chinese economy is allowing for its comparative advantage in many labour intensive goods to shift to lower cost economies in the region like Vietnam and Cambodia. The SAFTA dummy coefficient is low in value and is not significant indicating the weak trade creating tendencies of the regional trading arrangement. The author however draws his conclusions based on available evidence from some other studies and trends that show a slow increase in intra-regional trade in South Asia, to say that there is scope and hope for the RTA to show a positive performance and enhance intra-regional trade. The fixed effects and random effects models while giving expected signs for the trade restrictiveness coefficients also reverse the sign for SAFTA. The OTRI has a negative coefficient as expected. Overall the study does not show any significantly positive impact of SAFTA on intra-regional trade in South Asia.

The advancements in the gravity model specification and alternative formulation and estimation methodologies notwithstanding, the verdict on the benefits of SAFTA remains inconclusive.

As tariffs have come down through multilateral or preferential trade agreements further intra-regional trade enhancement will be possible only if the open ended reforms in NTBs become the primary agenda for South Asian economies. Trade facilitation, that is simplification of trade procedures, is one mode to accomplish this task. The gravity model has been used to estimate the potential for trade enhancement in response to cost reduction when trade facilitation measures are adopted by individual countries or the region as a whole. Wilson and Otsuki (2007) have explored South Asian trade facilitation measures and found that if South Asia and the rest of the world were to raise their level of trade facilitation to half of the East Asian average, the gains to the region would be approximately US$36 billion. Out of those gains, about 87 per cent of the total would be generated from South Asia's own efforts (leaving the rest of the world unchanged). In an earlier study Wilson *et al.* (2005) have used the gravity model with a sample of 75 countries, to show that improved trade facilitation could increase trade by 10 per cent or US$377 billion.

Rahman *et al.* (2013) undertake a sector specific study to estimate the significance of trade facilitation for enhancing intra-regional trade in the textile and clothing sector using a gravity model. The textiles and clothing sector is one of the most important and leading export sectors for South Asian countries and in 2011, textiles and clothing exports from Bangladesh were 92 per cent of the total exports (US$22 billion), while India exported US$29.5 billion (9.5%), Pakistan US$13.5 billion (50%), Sri Lanka US$4.3 billion (44%) and Nepal US$203 million (67%), respectively. Given its significance for regional economies the textiles and clothing should be a prime mover in promoting regional trade. In the past, barriers—tariff as well as non-tariff—have however been responsible for the low shares that this sector has in regional exports. The authors use a standard gravity model with representative variables for trade facilitation as captured by the World Bank Logistics Performance Index (LPI), cost to import and export, the number of days to export, number of documents required for export and customs efficiency in the estimable equation. The OLS estimation results show that trade in South Asia is sensitive to the cost of import and export, number of documents, number of days to export and import and customs infrastructure. The number of documents is not among the most significant variables where cost reduction would lead to trade enhancement.

In another study De (2011) makes an attempt to identify trade barriers for India's services trade. This study uses an augmented gravity model with a three-stage regression process to understand the impact of the services trade facilitation indicators. With initial specifications undertaken with standard gravity variables, subsequent regressions that include, one at a time, the set of services trade facilitation indicators show partner country's air transportation infrastructure, information and technology quality, regulatory quality, and overall competitiveness to be statistically significant. The coefficients for these trade facilitation indicators are then used to create a composite measure of trade facilitation. The gravity equation is then re-estimated with this composite trade facilitation indicator. The estimated results show that 1 per cent improvement in services trade facilitation measures would lead to a 2 per cent rise in services export in India. At the same time, India's partner countries' services trade infrastructure is relatively better and positively associated with services import. Hence, exporting country's services trade infrastructure is more important than that of importing country.

3.3.3 India and Pan Asian Economic Integration

The ambiguous results on the benefits of SAFTA and the underlying flaws in its design with respect to trade enhancing measures of trade facilitation and positive list delineation have led to India looking elsewhere as regards the prospect of economic integration. India has actively followed the policy of Looking East, a decision that was aimed at the time of its initiation in 1991 at taking advantage of the experience of the South East/East Asian economies experience of economic reforms and that more recently, in the wake of global and regional developments, has acquired the additional dimension of regionalism. The first formal economic institutional move in this direction has been the free trade agreement with ASEAN that has been operational since 2010. The framework FTA agreement with ASEAN was announced in 2003 and finally signed after six years of protracted negotiations in 2009. The agreement, which is for trade in goods only, provides for elimination of tariffs on about 80 per cent of bilaterally traded goods by 2016. India's FTA, owing to the prolonged negotiations, has also placed it at a late-mover disadvantage with respect to China in the ASEAN market which has an earlier entry into the ASEAN market through its FTA. The evaluation of the extent of late-mover disadvantage using the RCA index has already been discussed in an earlier section in this monograph. India's compromise in the goods FTA may be attributed to two aspects. One, the subsequent FTAs in services and investment liberalisation were expected to result in more favourable outcomes given India's greater advantages in these sectors; and two, there were growing regional compulsions. The latter has probably been a more important factor as China's FTA in goods was already operational and expected to be effective from January 2010, while the other components of the comprehensive economic cooperation pact, that is, agreements for investment and services liberalisation, had also been signed. Over this time, Korea and Japan had also signed FTAs with ASEAN. Therefore, India could not afford to lose any more time. The FTA has placed India on an equal footing with the other regional economies, thereby giving it a legitimate right to play a more appropriate role in the regional economic order. The FTA also formalises India's relationship with ASEAN, which is the accepted regional focal point for economic integration for a Pan Asian economic community as envisioned by the 16 member East Asian Summit (EAS) (Batra, 2010). While the analysis for individual FTAs with ASEAN has been undertaken in terms of relative comparative advantage structures, this section is focused on the Asian economic community that is projected to be the outcome of this initiative. In accordance with this vision the 2011 summit of the EAS proposed the RCEP (regional comprehensive economic partnership) among the member economies. Given the huge scope of tariff and non-tariff reduction and removal among member economies, this formation appears to hold considerable potential for trade creation. The RCEP has also provided a feasible forum for India and China to come together in a regional trade arrangement.[9] While the negotiations for RCEP have only just begun and the gains and benefits are yet to be evaluated, some earlier studies with respect to the constituent elements of the emerging regional order may be relevant to the context.

Bhattacharya and Bhattacharyay (2007) present an interesting analysis of the bilateral trade between India and China using a gravity model. The focus of the analysis is on the potential gains and losses of a preferential trading arrangement between the two countries. While the possibility of India and China entering into a formal bilateral free trade arrangement may be remote, analytical interest in the scope and potential of such an arrangement is worthy of estimation given the rapidity with which trade between these two nations has gathered momentum and volume. Evidence towards this trend is given by the authors and they state that in 2004-05, China became the third largest importer of Indian goods next to USA and UAE. USA's share in India's exports was 16.74 per cent, while that of UAE was 8.96 per cent and for China it was 5.79 per cent in 2004-05 having increased from near oblivion in 2000-01. Similarly, in imports, for which China was almost a non-entity a few years back, there has been incredible progress in its market penetration in India. China emerged as the largest exporter to Indian market surpassing traditional partners like USA and UK. In 2004-05, China's share in India's total imports was 6.30%, the highest among all trading partners, followed by USA with a share of 5.88 per cent. Their study is a comparative-

9. India and China are otherwise participants in the Bangkok Agreement (now called the Asia Pacific Trade Agreement), an inter-sub regional integration arrangement. India has been a member of the since 1975 and China joined in 2000. The limited scope and coverage of the concessions offered under the agreement makes it rather ineffective in taking forward the idea of regional economic architecture in Asia.

static analysis showing the tentative increase in bilateral trade due to PTAs and FTA between India and China. The authors have used the gravity formulation of Srinivasan and Canonero (S-C) who have estimated the effects of PTAs on South Asian countries. In this study, the model which was adopted by Srinivasan and Canonero (1993; 1995) has been relied upon. Given the estimated parametric value of tariff barriers from the fitted regression equations of the aggregated commodity groups, and changes in tariff rates under different alternative scenarios, the percentage increase in import from China to India and percentage increase in exports from India to China have been worked out. Simulating the impact of PTAs and FTA, the products/product groups at the 2-digit HS levels have been taken aggregating from the 8-digit level. Alternative hypothetical scenarios are constructed for analysis. The results are in conformity with prior expectations that the gains of an FTA in the initial period would accrue to the country with lower initial tariffs.

In an interesting analysis Bussiere and Mehl (2008), compare and contrast the growth paths and trade integration patterns of India and China. Using a gravity model the authors assess the 'natural' overall degree of trade intensity and strength of bilateral trade linkages of India and China. The gravity model is formulated to estimate a benchmark trade level against which the actual levels are then gauged. The estimated gravity model has the size of bilateral trade of country-pairs expressed as a function of the real GDP, bilateral distance and a set of dummy variables representing participation of FTAs, common language, shared borders and common history. As regards the overall level of trade intensity their results suggest that China is already highly integrated relative to fundamentals (explanatory variables) while India is relatively poorly integrated relative to fundamentals. China is well integrated with the Asian economies relative to what the fundamentals warrant, reflecting, according to the authors, its insertion into the regional production network of exports. China is also seen to be well integrated with other commodity exporters like Canada, Peru and Australia. India, in contrast, has weaker integration with Asian economies relative to fundamentals. Further, the authors using the RCA indices show the differential placement of the two economies along the technological ladder. Classifying the exports according to their technical intensity (high tech, medium-low-tech, medium-high-tech and low tech; based on CEPII classification), they state that share of China's high tech goods in total exports has increased from 12 to 35 per cent while the share of low tech goods declined from 63 to 32 per cent over the reference period of 1993-2005. At variance with the trends for China, low tech goods continue to occupy more than half of India's exports and high tech have only a 5 per cent share. Except for pharmaceuticals Indian exports do not exhibit strength in any other high tech categories. The trade trends are supported by an assessment of competitiveness that is undertaken in the same study using the Balasssa index of RCA. The results of RCA support the conclusion that China has a clear comparative advantage in the high tech sector even while it continues to have a strong comparative advantage in low tech goods as well. In contrast, India has RCA in the medium and especially low tech categories. China's comparative advantage is closer to the more developed countries as also to the other Asian economies that are a part of the Asian production networks. India's RCA is closer to other emerging economies like Brazil, Russia, Turkey and Tunisia.

Yu (2011) is an exercise using a gravity model for the ASEAN-China-India countries to examine the theoretical proposition of the H-O model that a capital abundant country would export capital intensive commodities in accordance with its comparative advantage. To incorporate the H-O theoretical proposition Yu develops a variable called difference of capital-labour ratio to capture the difference of economy-wide capital-labour ratio between exporter and importer countries. Given that an exporter if more capital-abundant than the importer, as per the H-O model would export more capital-intensive goods, Yu drops those labour-abundant exportable goods from the regress and, in particular, the labour-intensive goods, that is, SITC code 0, 1, 2, 3, 4, and 9, are dropped from his estimations. The expected sign of the coefficient of the difference variable is positive, higher the difference of capital-labour ratios, the more capital intensive commodities the ACI (ASEAN, the People's Republic of China and India) countries export. After several robustness checks,

OLS doesn't give the expected sign but when the country-pair specific fixed effects and year-specific fixed effects are controlled for, as also the multilateral resistance and time varying country fixed effects while avoiding the possible bias of zero trade values and the PPML estimation is undertaken, Yu finds the coefficient has a positive sign hence supporting the H-O proposition in his estimation of the gravity model for the ACI region.

Veeramani and Saini (2011) makes a quantitative assessment of the trade impact in the plantation sector of the ASEAN-India FTA (AIFTA) using a gravity model framework. The likely negative impact of the AIFTA on plantation commodities was at the core of the prolonged negotiations for the FTA. Separate gravity models, augmented by tariff levels have been estimated for coffee, tea and pepper. Estimation is undertaken using trade data for the year 2007 on export flows (current US$) from the COMTRADE-WITS for a large number of reporting countries to about 225 partner counties. Import tariff data is for the years 2007, 2006 or 2005 depending on the availability for individual countries. Estimation is undertaken using a Tobit model with two regressions, for each commodity, using simple average and weighted average tariff rates. As expected, both the tariff variables yield statistically significant negative signs for all the commodities. The point estimates suggest that the elasticity of imports with respect to tariff is the highest for coffee, followed by tea and pepper.

3.3.4 Hidden Costs of Trading and NTBs

In economic trade theory it is generally assumed that international political considerations are "transient and random in nature" and therefore, safely ignored relative to long run market factors (Mcmillan, 1997). Some studies, though in a different context, have attempted to include political context in the gravity analysis. Noland (2005) examines the role of public attitudes towards foreign countries in bilateral trade. Public attitudes as a reflection of trust, cultural affinities and political ideologies may impact to some extent, transaction costs of trade. Noland examines the impact of American public attitudes toward foreign countries, referred to as 'affinity' on the volume of trade. Specifically the analysis relates to the question of whether popular attitudes, as elicited by periodical surveys of the Chicago Council of Foreign Relations (CCFR), convey any information about trust, risk, or transactions costs beyond what can be explained through standard economic models. The gravity model estimation is constrained to bilateral trade between the United States and its partners by the availability of the attitudinal data collected by the CCFR. Moreover, the attitudinal data are for the US only and there are no reciprocal data on foreign attitudes toward the US. While the author states that it would be preferable to be able to observe the attitudes of both parties, the data is limited to only one sided reflection of attitudes. The gravity model is estimated with the dependent variable as log non-fuel trade. Affinity is included as a 'temperature' variable indicative of the extent of warmth in the bilateral relationship. The estimation results show the coefficient of 'temperature' to be positive implying warmer feelings are associated with more trade. The size and statistical significance of the estimated coefficient varies with the size of the sample number of countries. Inclusion/exclusion of countries like Iran lead to significant variation in the magnitude of impact of affinity on trade. Noland describes this as an unavoidable by-product of the small and from an economic perspective idiosyncratic country sample covered by the CCFR survey.

In the Indian context, Pradhan (2006) has used the variable 'trading affinity' in his gravity estimation for a similar effect. Pradhan has used an augmented gravity model to analyse India's world export flows and the coefficients thus obtained are incorporated to predict India's export potential to the six-member GCC countries, namely, Bahrain, Kuwait, Oman, Qatar, Saudi Arabia, and United Arab Emirates (UAE). This model has been estimated using the OLS technique with panel data. With a dependent variable as India's total merchandise exports, the gravity model is estimated in log-linear form between country-pairs of India with other 150 countries of the world for the period, 1994-2004, with an additional explanatory variable for trading affinity apart from the standard gravity and proximity variables. The trading affinity is incorporated as a dummy that is constructed on the basis of more than one per cent share of partner countries in India's total trade for the estimation period. Countries with an average of more than one percent share in India's total trade for the period 1994 to 2004 continuously would have a value of unity and 0 otherwise. The estimated coefficient for the dummy trade affinity index shows a positive sign and a value of more than 1, indicating that countries having traditional trading affinity as in the case of India-GCC, they are likely to trade more.

3.4.4.1 Conflict and Political Economy Variables in the Gravity Model

The normally accepted instruments of NTBs used by India, South Asian economies in general and globally have been often held responsible for the huge gap between potential and actual trade among South Asian economies and particularly India and Pakistan. It has also simultaneously been known and accepted by economic analysts, trade specialists, policy makers that the biggest impediment or NTB to trade potential being realised between India and Pakistan is the underlying political conflict between the two nations. Relatively fewer studies have been undertaken to estimate the trade costs of conflict in comparison with the large number of studies undertaken to calculate the trade benefits associated with tariff reduction and NTB elimination. A quantitative analysis of this barrier to trade has been undertaken by Batra (2013).

Batra (2013) has undertaken the first ever comprehensive, technical analysis of the trade-conflict relationship in the South Asian context with India-Pakistan conflict as the core backdrop of the analysis. Batra (2013) extends the gravity model in Batra (2004) by including representative variables for political influences and conflict with its multiple dimensions, that is, bilateral conflict, violence or warfare that individual countries in a trading pair maybe involved in with third countries, civil conflict as well as the expectation of conflict. The last is a reflection of the South Asian situation where persistent and long standing India-Pakistan conflict not only dominates the regional landscape but also lends to it an atmosphere of constant anticipation of conflict. The model is estimated for a global sample for the period 1965-2000. The time period is inclusive of the major conflicts in South Asia and precedes the global change in security perceptions as an outcome of the 9/11 terrorist attacks in US, as also a slowdown in economic reforms across the developing world. Within the reference period analysis is also undertaken for the post 1991 sub-period taking note of the systemic economic reforms towards liberalisation in India, other South Asian economies and developing countries all over the world. A sub-sample estimation is also undertaken for South Asia and specifically for the India-Pakistan dyad.

The estimation has been undertaken using panel data set. The gravity model estimates with panel data has also been undertaken using country pair fixed effects (CPFE-within) only as well as CPFE with time dummies. Results are qualitatively similar across model variations. The direction of causality from conflict to trade is considered appropriate with reference to the South Asian contextual reality. Econometric robustness has been ensured by using alternative methodologies and variables. Apart from the satisfactory performance of the model with regard to standard gravity variables as also the proximity variables, the results are enlightening in terms of the costs that the South Asian region has had to pay for persistent conflict between India and Pakistan. The conflict variable as expected has a negative and significant coefficient with an implied cost in terms of 68 per cent loss in bilateral trade. Anticipated conflict adds to the costs and implies a cost of 65 per cent in terms of bilateral trade. The other interesting result is obtained with regard to the border. The estimation results show that the positive effect of common border on bilateral trade is magnified as the number of states with which the border is shared increases but the same effect is negated if the countries sharing a border are also in conflict. In the smaller South Asian sub sample it is observed that as against theoretical expectations and in a reversal of the full sample results, a common border acts more as a barrier than facilitator for trade and implies costs to the extent of a 52 per cent loss in bilateral trade. The negative impact of conflict is further confirmed when estimation is undertaken by addition of explicit conflict variables in the regression. On thus netting out the impact of conflict the border variable acquires a positive coefficient but with negligible statistical significance.

The India-Pakistan sub sample estimations, even though highly constrained in terms of the number of observations, further confirm these results. In the analysis on the gap between actual and potential trade levels the estimation results are per *a priori* expectations. The rival pair with maximum gap between actual and potential levels of trade is India and Pakistan in the years 1995 and 2000, a period of heightened tensions that culminated in a warlike conflict in 1999 over the longest standing territorial dispute over Kashmir between the two countries. Even though in a constrained sample, the results reveal a dilution of the distance effect in face of historical enmities, an aspect that though highlighted by Frankel (1997) was considered to be outweighed by the border effect. Frankel in fact raises the question of the impact on trade, of geographical units that are not just politico-military alliances, but political unions. While there has been some notable analysis for intra-national trade in Canada,[10] extension to likely effects of political integration or disintegration among members of an economic union on international trade remains an issue for future research.

10. McCallum(1995) and Helliwell (1996) applied the gravity model to trade among Canadian provinces and American states to find that provinces that lie in the same country have around 20 times greater tendency to trade with each other than if they have a border between them.

4

Conclusions

This monograph has undertaken to present the empirical evidence towards the evolution of India's RCA (revealed comparative advantage) patterns and regional economic integration strategy in the post economic liberalisation period. The evidence presented against a brief theoretical background, is focused on three broad issues viz., structure of RCA, trade potential and regional integration. Drawing upon existing research on these issues the analysis presents evidence for the last two decades with regard to both merchandise and services trade from the Indian perspective. Data limitations in the services trade analysis have also been highlighted in the appropriate context. Wherever relevant, the evidence for the Chinese economy has also been presented to highlight the simultaneous though differential developments of the two most dynamic economies in the world. Broad conclusions that thus emerge from the analysis are discussed below.

Analysis for the RCA in the Indian context has been presented as undertaken at the aggregate sector level as well as more detailed commodity level mostly using the standard Balassa index. The calculations show that in the year 2000 irrespective of the level of classification, India enjoys maximum advantage in the category of manufactures chiefly by material followed by agriculture and allied products. Furthermore, it is observed that the advantage at the aggregate sector level may be at variance with that enjoyed by India at the commodity level. Sectors that rank among the top 10 according to the value of the index of RCA are not necessarily able to retain their position when ranked according to comparative advantage at the 6-digit constituent commodity level. No other sector, other than cotton that ranks among the top 10 according to the value of the index of RCA retains its comparative ranking at the dis-aggregated level. Simultaneously, there are also some sectors where India may be disadvantageously placed at the aggregate level but may enjoy comparative advantage at the constituent commodity level. At the 6- digit level of classification, the commodities that rank among the top 100 according to the index of RCA while being dispersed across various sectors, are largely drawn from sectors like organic chemicals, cotton, salt, sulphur, earth, stone, plaster, lime and cement and iron and steel in India. Given the fact that actual trade takes place at the commodity level, results at the dis-aggregated level are more meaningful and relevant.

Inter-temporal analysis shows relative stability in the structure of comparative advantage for the manufacturing sector irrespective of the length of the time period under consideration. Longer time periods from the mid-1980s to the 2000s or from 2000 to more recent years in the decade do not show the RCA to have undergone a significant structural change. Structural change is however evident for sectors within manufacturing. Maximum structural change is experienced by sectors like other base metals, cermet, articles thereof, ships, boats and other floating structures and fertilisers. Sectors which have remained structurally same in India are organic chemicals, tanning, dyeing extracts, tannins, derivs, pigments etc., carpets and other textile floor coverings and footwear, gaiters and the like, parts thereof. Relative to China, in both the years for which analysis is undertaken, that is 2000 and 2003, sectors where only India is advantageously placed lie predominantly in the agriculture and allied products category. This advantage has been further consolidated in the year 2003. The other category where India consolidates its comparative position vis-à-vis China in the global market is resource based manufactures and also miscellaneous manufactures. Future research ought to extend the inter-temporal exercise in a comparative framework over a longer period of time. This would help shed light on the extent of dynamism evident in the structure of comparative advantage which could contribute to policy formulation in the areas of trade policy and enhancing manufacturing sector capabilities in India.

When compared with other South Asian countries over the longer period of 1993-2004, it is observed that India has been slow to register a change in its structure of comparative advantage. In the period 2004-2006 relative to that in 1991-1993, India's comparative advantage structure is seen to have gained competitiveness relative to other SAARC economies in products like dyes, pharmaceuticals, yarn etc. Product categories in which the four South Asian economies (India, Bangladesh, Pakistan, and Sri Lanka) enjoy comparative advantage include commodities like textiles, shrimps, spices, woven carpets, cotton yarn wastes etc. China in contrast has shown the maximum change in the Southeast and East Asian region over the same period.

The analysis according to factor intensity reveals comparative advantage for manufacturing sector to be predominantly in the labour and resource intensive manufactures for India. Sectors like textiles (yarn, fabric, made-up articles n.e.s and related products) and articles of apparel and clothing accessories dominate in these categories. The next largest category is that of manufactures that makes a high demand for skill, technology, capital and scale. Organic chemicals followed by inorganic chemicals occupy a predominant position in this category. At a more disaggregated level, the comparative advantage is observed to be in the unskilled labour intensive commodity category. Science-based industries contribute less than 10 per cent of the comparative advantage in the manufacturing sector in India. While the pattern for China reveals substantial similarities, in absolute terms China's science-based industries are almost double the number in India. In the Indian context, the category of medicinal and pharmaceutical products is predominant while in China the category photographic apparatus, equipment and optical goods dominates. In the leading science-based commodity categories, China enjoys more than double the comparative advantage that India enjoys in the same category. It is also noted that high technology manufactured products like electronic goods while having moved up the ranking of sectors with comparative advantage enjoyed by China, does not figure in the sectors where India enjoys comparative advantage in the global market. Even for sectors where there is an overlapping advantage for India and China, the latter holds a far larger share of the world market in comparison with India. This in fact is true for China even in case of sectors for which the ranking has slipped to a lower position like in case of railway products and equipment.

The pattern of RCA has also been analysed for the extent of competition that India and China may pose for each other in the global market. However it is observed that despite the similarity in structure of comparative advantage, there is no correlation between the manufacturing sectors of India and China in the global economy. Within manufacturing though, India and China have a competitive relationship in organic chemicals, inorganic chemicals sectors that make a high demand for capital, skill, technology, and scale, the resource intensive category of non-metallic mineral manufactures, n.e.s. and in manufactures of metals, n.e.s which is a low capital, skill, scale and technology commodity category. On the other hand, a complementary relationship is evident in labour and resource intensive sectors like textile yarn, fabrics, made-up articles, n.e.s and related products and articles of apparel and clothing accessories.

The element of competition has also been examined across sub-regions given that both India and China have signed trade agreements with ASEAN. The RCA analysis indicates that India is likely to be outcompeted by China in some of its top ranking sectors like coffee, tea, mate and spices, silk, iron and steel and glass and glassware among others in the ASEAN market owing to a prior entry by China through its FTA (Free Trade Agreement) with the 10 member regional association. At the commodity level, India is likely to be overtaken in sectors like manmade staple fibres, tools, implements, cutlery etc. of base metal and nuclear reactors, boilers, machinery etc. by China. These are sectors/commodities where even though India has experienced an increase in its market share in ASEAN, the Chinese increase is double that of India. In sectors like organic chemicals, articles of iron and steel, rubber products there are some commodities where India may have a higher comparative advantage but is still potentially likely to be threatened by China on account of its prior implementation of the FTA with ASEAN. There are also sectors like cotton, where India and China are equally competitive therefore pose a threat to each other in an equal number of commodities.

India's comparative advantage, in most of the important agricultural exports has been found to be eroding and/or losing out to other Asian competitors in certain commodities like tea, coffee, cashew and spices. In case of marine products, the dominant position among India's agricultural exports is not attributable to India's comparative advantage in the global markets but to a growing demand for these products among the international consumers.

As regards individual country members of ASEAN, some studies have shown that RCA structure of Thailand and Philippines has a high, positive and statistically significant correlation with that of India and China. An FTA between these economies with correlated and hence competitive comparative advantage would therefore not be gainful. India's negotiations with Thailand for an FTA though announced in 2003 have not progressed beyond the EHP (early harvest programme) with 84 commodities precisely for this reason. Domestic producers in India have been wary of the possible competition that cheaper imports from Thailand would introduce in India through the FTA. The analysis at the aggregate level however needs to be supplemented with a more detailed commodity level calculation of the comparative advantage enjoyed by individual countries in the relevant markets. Some studies that have undertaken the analysis at a more detailed level for the period 1990-2007 show India's advantage to be in knowledge based industry of chemical products while the advantage in textiles is likely to face stiff competition from China in the post MFA-phase out scenario.

In the more recent studies, the traditional RCA calculations have been questioned and re-evaluated. In the wake of global financial crisis, as the trade imbalances and surpluses are analysed, it is being realised that the true value of RCA, particularly for the economies that are highly integrated in the global value chains, may be lower than that reflected in the trade statistics. The traditional measure of RCA based on a country's trade data may therefore distort the competitiveness ranking among nations. China is one of the most deeply integrated countries in the global value chain.

In particular it is shown by some studies that in case of China, its own value addition/comparative advantage in sectors that are more sophisticated or high skilled like computers, electronic devices, and telecommunication equipment, is not as distinct as is evident on the basis of RCA calculations using the traditional Balassa index.

Studies on India's RCA in trade in services though limited in number and constrained by data deficiencies reveal a very strong RCA for the computer and information services sector ahead of countries like Ireland, Israel, UK, and Finland. Computer and information service exports are also revealed as an important sector of the Indian economy. India is observed to have achieved comparative advantage in financial, and computer and information services over the period 1991-2005, while having lost advantage in traditional sectors such as transport and travel services. Overall too, over the period 1994 to 2003 India's comparative advantage is observed to have increased. Over the same period, China's RCA index value in services is shown to have declined. China, in general, reveals little comparative advantage in service exports.

As regards India's trade potential, this has been identified using the gravity model that explains the flow of trade between a pair of countries as being proportional to their economic 'mass' (national income) and inversely proportional to the distance between them. The set of explanatory variables in most studies have been expanded beyond income and distance to include indicators of geographic, historical, linguistic and cultural proximity and affinity—all factors that would naturally enhance bilateral trade. Additional policy variables such as membership of free trade agreements, level of tariffs and indicators of hidden trade barriers and costs that impact trade flows have also been included in some analysis of the pattern of India's bilateral trade and potential expansion possibilities. Gravity model estimations have been undertaken for both, cross section and panel data accounting simultaneously for the several advancements in econometric methodology.

Almost all estimation results show the gravity equation to fit the data well and deliver precise and plausible income and distance elasticities as also estimates for other geographical and historical characteristics. Alternative measures of GNP (gross national product) in terms of current dollar value and PPP (purchasing power parity) do not alter either the sign or significance of different explanatory variables.

With bilateral trade data for the year 2000, the estimates of India's global trade potential reveal that the magnitude of India's trade potential is maximum for the Asia-Pacific region followed by Western Europe, North America, Middle East, Central and Eastern Europe and Latin America. In Asia, Japan, Pakistan, China, Philippines and Korea reveal maximum potential for expansion of trade with India. Among the set of countries comprising the EU, India has trade potential with all except Belgium. In North America both the US and Canada reveal considerable potential for expanding trade. In Central and Eastern Europe, Poland, has the maximum potential for expansion of trade with India. For the CIS (Commonwealth of Independent States) region, the estimates indicate India's trade with the region as a whole as also with member countries like Russia, Ukraine, and Belarus has exceeded the potential.

As regards regional groupings India's trade potential is examined for SAARC (South Asian Association for Regional Cooperation), ASEAN (Association of Southeast Asian Nations) and GCC (Gulf Cooperation Council). In case of SAARC, not surprisingly, the maximum trade potential, well beyond the actual levels, is indicated with Pakistan. For ASEAN, high trade potential is indicated for Philippines, Vietnam, and Cambodia. Countries in ASEAN with which India's trade is in excess of potential include Singapore, Malaysia, and Indonesia. Among the countries of the GCC, potential is indicated with Oman, Kuwait, and Qatar. Among specific country groupings/ trade arrangements India's trade potential is maximum with Pakistan in SAARC, with Philippines and Cambodia in the ASEAN region and with Oman, Qatar, and Kuwait in the GCC. Outside of regions and regional groupings, the India-China bilateral trade stands out as having a vast potential for expansion. The common membership of PTAs (preferential trade agreements) further enhances this potential. Most studies reiterate this pattern of potential for India's trade with its major partner countries.

As regards India's trade agreements, with the exception of India's CECA (Comprehensive Economic Cooperation Agreement) with Singapore and the more recent trade agreements with Japan and Korea which have been in the nature of comprehensive agreements covering liberalisation of trade in goods, select services and investment, the many FTAs that India has signed and/or participated in, are classified as shallow and attain less than the average grade in terms of incorporating best practices for such arrangements.

India's membership of the regional FTA, SAFTA (South Asian Free Trade Area), has been analysed in terms of both the trade creation impact of the FTA on the member countries as well as the implications of economic asymmetry among the member nations. That India is the largest and most dynamic economy in the SAFTA provides scope for differential potential benefits of the regional FTA. The SAFTA is therefore examined to not just review its efficiency implications but also in the context of prevailing fears among the smaller economies of the region of trade gains from preferential access accruing to the larger economy, i.e., India. Estimations undertaken with alternative country sets in the region for trade creation and diversion effects of SAPTA (SAARC Preferential Trading Arrangement) and SAFTA have not yielded any definitive results. While most indicate that a regional trading arrangement in South Asia would be potentially trade creating for a subset of the member countries, the composition of the sub-set varies across these studies. Gravity model based studies show that the gap between actual trade and potential trade may be reduced by elimination of tariffs but not fully. The full potential can be attained only if other factors like NTBs (non-tariff barriers) and political constraints are taken care of. The country pairs with maximum gap between potential and actual trade are India-Pakistan and India-Bangladesh. It is noteworthy that Pakistan and Bangladesh are the two south Asian countries that do not as yet have a formal trade agreement with India.

Trade costs of the underlying political conflict between India and Pakistan have been estimated in a recent study using the traditional gravity model that is further augmented by including representative variables for political influences and conflict in its multiple dimensions. The analysis using the conflict augmented gravity model for the period 1965-2000 for a global and South Asian sub sample of countries shows that the positive effect of common border on bilateral trade is magnified as the number of states with which the border is shared increases but the same effect is negated if the countries sharing a border are also in conflict. The result is a clear reflection of trade trends in South Asia. The results also bring to the fore the fact that in South Asia as against theoretical expectations and in a reversal of the full sample results, a common border acts more as a barrier than facilitator for trade and implies costs to the extent of a 52 per cent loss in bilateral trade. The negative impact of conflict is further confirmed when estimation is undertaken by addition of explicit conflict variables in the regression equation.

Beyond its participation in the regional FTA, India has actively followed the policy of Looking East, a decision that was aimed at the time of its initiation in 1991 at taking advantage of the experience of the South East/East Asian economies' experience of economic reforms and that more recently, in the wake of global and regional developments, has acquired the additional dimension of regionalism. India's FTA with ASEAN has formalised the economic relationship with ASEAN, which in turn is accepted as the regional focal point for a Pan Asian economic community envisioned by the 16 member East Asian Summit (EAS). While the analysis for individual country FTAs of the +3 economies with ASEAN has been undertaken in terms of relative comparative advantage structures and the extent of overlap and hence competitive tendencies in some studies, welfare and efficiency implications of the economic community formation have not been examined. Given recent developments whereby the EAS has in its 2011 summit proposed the RCEP (regional comprehensive economic partnership) among the member economies, this would be a useful research subject in the coming years. That the RCEP also provides a feasible forum for India and China to come together in a regional trade arrangement is another dimension worthy of analysis. As negotiations for RCEP have only just begun with first round held in 2013 the gains and benefits are yet to be evaluated. Some earlier studies with respect to the constituent elements of the emerging regional order may be considered relevant to the context. Comparative-static analysis and alternative hypothetical scenarios show a tentative increase in bilateral trade due to PTA and FTA between India and China and that, the gains of an FTA in the initial period would accrue to the country with lower initial tariffs.

Summing up, it may be stated that the rapid pace of India's trade integration with the global economy since economic liberalisation was initiated in 1991 has not necessarily been accompanied by an equally rapid pace of diversification of its underlying structure of comparative advantage, particularly in merchandise trade. Both in the context of South Asia and across Southeast/East Asia, India has been among the slow moving nations along the ladder of technological up-gradation and in the process of global/regional value chain evolution. In terms of regional trade agreements and its trade agreements strategy, India has been an active participant both within South Asia and in Asia as a whole. However, the increasing number of FTAs has not been necessarily or unambiguously beneficial particularly given the relatively lower levels of dynamism of India's comparative advantage structure. In South Asia, the persistent nature of India-Pakistan conflict continues to impose significant trade costs on the region.

References

Abraham, Filip and Jan van Hove (2005). "The Rise of China: Prospects of Regional Trade Policy," *Review of World Economics (Weltwirtschaftliches Archiv)* 141(3): 486-509, October. Springer

Akhter, Naseem and Ejaz Ghani (2010). "Regional Integration in South Asia: An Analysis of Trade Flows Using the Gravity Model", *The Pakistan Development Review* 49(2), Summer.

Amighini, A., M. Leone and R. Rabellotti (2011). "Persistence versus Change in the International Specialization Pattern of Italy: how much does the 'Direct Effect' Matter?", *Regional Studies* 45: 381-401.

Amiti, M. (1999). "Specialization Patterns in Europe", *Weltwirtschaftliches Archiv* 135: 573-93.

Anderson, K. and R.G. Garnaut (1980). "Asean Export Specialization and the Evolution of Comparative Advantage in the Western Pacific Region", in R.G. Garnaut (ed.), *ASEAN in a Chainging Pacific and World Economy.* Australian National University Press.

Anderson, James E. and Eric van Wincoop (2003). "Gravity with Gravitas: A Solution to the Border Puzzle", *American Economic Review* 93(1): 170-92.

Ariovich, G. (1979). "The Comparative Advantage of South Africa as Revealed by Export Shares", *South African Journal of Economics* 47(2): 188-97.

Asian Development Bank (ADB) (2008). *Quantification of Benefits from Economic Cooperation in South Asia.* Macmillan India Ltd.

Baier, Scott L. and Jeffrey H. Bergstrand (2002). *On the Endogeneity of International Trade Flows and Free Trade Agreements*, American Economic Association Annual Meeting.

Balassa, Bela (1965). "Trade Liberalization and "Revealed" Comparative Advantage", *The Manchester School of Economic & Social Studies* 33: 99-123.

———. (1977). "'Revealed' Comparative Advantage Revisited: An Analysis of Relative Export Shares of the Industrial Countries, 1953-1971", *The Manchester School of Economic & Social Studies* 45(4): 327-44.

———. (1979). "The "Stages" Approach to Comparative Advantage", in Irma Adelman (ed.), *Economic Growth and Resources.* Volume 4: National and International Issues. London: MacMillan)

———. (1986). "Comparative Advantage in Manufactured Goods: A Reappraisal", *The Review of Economics and Statistics* 68(2): 315-19.

Baldwin, Richard and Taglioni, Daria (2006). "Gravity for Dummies and Dummies for Gravity Equation", *CEPR Discussion Papers* 5850.

Ballance, Robert, H. Forstner and T. Murray (1985). "On Measuring Comparative Advantage: A Note on Bowen´s Indices", *Weltwirtschaftliches Archiv* 121: 346-50.

———. (1986). "More on Measuring Comparative Advantage: A Reply", *Weltwirtschaftliches Archiv* 122: 375-78.

———. (1987). "Consistency Tests of Alternative Measures of Comparative Advantage", *Review of Economics and Statistics* 69: 157-61.

Barattieri, Alessandro (2011). *Comparative Advantage, Services Trade and Global Imbalances.* Third Conference of GIST. Stockholm

Batra, Amita (2004). "India's Global Trade Potential: The Gravity Model Approach", *ICRIER Working Paper* 151. New Delhi: ICRIER.

———. (2005). *India-Country Perspectives in South Asia Free Trade Area: Opportunities and Challenges*. Washington DC: USAID. pp.57-74

———. (2006). "Asian Economic Integration: ASEAN+3+1 or ASEAN+1s?", *ICRIER Working Paper* 186. New Delhi: ICRIER.

———. (2007). "The Structure of Comparative Advantage of China and India: Global and Regional Dynamics", *China & World Economy* 15(6), 15 November. Blackwell.

———. (2010). *Indo ASEAN Agreement Boosts India's Image' Policy Commentary.* Sigur Centre for Asian Studies, George Washington University. February

———. (2011). "Asian Economic Integration and Sub-Regionalism: A Case Study of BIMSTEC", *International Studies* 47(1). Sage.

———. (2013). *Regional Economic Integration in South Asia: Trapped in Conflict?* London: Routledge.

Batra, A. and Z. Khan (2005). "Revealed Comparative Advantage: An Analysis for India and China", *Working Paper* No. 168. New Delhi: ICRIER.

Bayoumi, Tamim (2011). *Changing Patterns of Global Trade*. International Monetary Fund.

Beck, T. (2003). "Financial Dependence and International Trade", *Review of International Economics* 11: 296-316.

Bergsten, C.F., C. Freeman N.R. Lardy and D.J. Mitchell (2008). *China's Rise: Challenges and Opportunities*. Washington D.C.: Peterson Institute of International Economics.

Bergstrand, Jeffrey H. (1985). "The Gravity Equation in International Trade: Some Microeconomic Foundations and Empirical Evidence", *The Review of Economics and Statistics* 67(3): 474-81, August. MIT Press.

Bhattacharyya, Ruma (2011). *Revealed Comparative Advantage and Competitiveness: A Case Study of India in Horticultural Products*. International Conference on Applied Economics.

Bhattacharya, S.K. (2004). "Does Bangladesh Benefit from Preferential Trade With India? A Gravity Analysis", *Economic and Political Weekly* 39(48): 5152-62.

Bhattacharya, Swapan K. and Biswa N. Bhattacharyay (2007). "Gains and Losses of India-China Trade Cooperation: A Gravity Model Impact Analysis", *CESifo Working Paper Series* No. 1970

Bhattacharyya, Ranajoy and Tathagata Banerjee (2006). "Does the Gravity Model Explain India's Direction of Trade? A Panel Data Approach", *Working Paper* No. 2006-09-01. Ahmedabad: Indian Institute of Management.

Bowen, H. (1983). "On the TheoreticalInterpretation of Indices of Trade Intensity and Revealed Comparative Advantage", *Weltwirtschaftliches Archiv* 119: 464-72.

———.(1985). "On Measuring Comparative Advantage: A Reply and Extensions", *Weltwirtschaftliches Archiv* 121(2): 351-54.

———. (1986). "On Measuring Comparative Advantage: Further Comments", *Weltwirtschaftliches Archiv* 122(2): 379-81.

Bowen, H.P., A. Hollander and J.-M. Viaene (1998). *Applied International Trade Analysis.* Houndmills and London: MacMillan.

Brander, James and Paul Krugman (1983). "A Reciprocal Dumping Model of International Trade", *Journal of International Economics* 15: 313-21. North-Holland

Bussiere, Matthieu and Arnaud Mehl (2008). "China's and India's Role in Global Trade and Finance: Twin Titans for the new Millenium", *European Central Bank Occasional Paper Series* No. 80/ January.

Carrere, C. (2003). "Revisiting the Effects of Regional Trading Agreements on Trade Flows with Proper Specification of the Gravity Model", *CERDI* 2003.10

Chor, D. (2008), "Unpacking Sources of Comparative Advantage: A Quantitative Approach", *Working Papers* No. 13-2008. Singapore Management University.

———. (2010). "Unpacking Sources of Comparative Advantage: A Quantitative Approach" *Journal of International Economics* 82(2): 152-67, November.

Costinot, A., D. Donaldson and I. Komunjer (2012). "What Goods do Countries trade? A Quantitative Exploration of Ricardo's Ideas", *Review of Economic Studies* 79: 581-608.

Cottey, Andrew (2009). "Sub-Regional Multilateralism in Europe: An Assessment", *EU4seas paper*. Barcelona: Barcelona Centre for International Studies. Retrieved from *www.cidob.org*

Coulibaly, S. (2004). "On the Assessment of Trade Creation and Trade Diversion Effects of Developing RTAs", Paper Presented at the *Annual Meeting 2005 of the Swiss Society of Economics and Statistics on Resource Economics, Technology, and Sustainable Development* .

Ciuriak, Dan, Beverly Lapham, Robert Wolfe, Terry Collins-William and John M. Curtis (2011). "New-New Trade Policy", *Queen's Economics Department Working Paper* No. 1263. Canada.

Chandran, Sarath B.P. (2010). "Trade Complementarity and Similarity between India and ASEAN Countries in the Context of the RTA", *MPRA Paper* 29279.

Daniels, H.E. (1950). "Rank Correlation and Population Models," *Journal of the Royal Statistical Society (Series B)* 12(2): 171-81.

Dasgupta, Dipak, Nihal Pitigala and Julien Gourdon (2012). "South Asia's Prospects from Global Rebalancing and Integration", in Philippa Dee (ed.), *Economic Reform Processes in South Asia: toward Policy Efficiency*. London: Routledge. pp.23-42.

De Benedictis, L. and M. Tamberi (2001). "Overall Specialization Empirics: Techniques and Applications", *Open Economies Review* 15: 323-46.

De, P. (2010). "Global Economic and Financial Crisis: India's Trade Potential and Prospects, and Implications for Asian Regional Integration", *Journal of Economic Integration* 25: 32-68.

———. (2011). "Assessing Barriers to Trade in Services in India", *Discussion Paper* 173. New Delhi: Research and Information Systems for Developing Countries (RIS).

De, Prabir and Ajitava Raychaudhuri (2008). "Is India's Services Trade Pro poor? A Simultaneous Approach", *Macao Regional Knowledge Hub Working Papers* No. 16. Macao University of Science and Technology and UNESCAP.

Deardorff, Alan (1995). "Determinants of Bilateral Trade: Does Gravity Work in a Classical World?" Paper presented at conference on *The Regionalization of the World Economy*. Woodstock, Vermont: NBER.

Djankov, Simeon, Rafael La Porta, Florencio Lopez-de-Silanes and Andrei Shleifer (2010). "Disclosure by Politicians", *American Economic Journal: Applied Economics* 2(2): 179-209, April. American Economic Association.

Egger P,. and M. Pfaffermayr (2003). "The Proper Panel Econometric Specification of the Gravity Equation: A Three-way Model with Bilateral Interaction Effects", *Empirical Economics* 28: 571-80.

Ferrarini, Benno and Pasquale Scaramozzino (2012). "Indicators and Patterns of Specialization in International Trade", *Working Paper* No. 2011/10. Swiss National Centre of Competence in Research.

Ferto, I. and J. Hubbard (2003). "Revealed Comparative Advantage and Competitiveness in Hungarian Agri-Food Sectors", *The World Economy* 26(2): 247-59.

Fourie. Johan and Dieter Von Fintel (2009). "World Rankings of Comparative Advantage in Service Exports", *Stellenbosch Economic Working Papers* 03/09. University of Stellenbosch.

Frankel, Jeffrey A (1997). *Regional Trading Blocs, Institute for International Economics*. Washington DC.

Frankel, J. and S-J. Wei (1997). "Regionalization of World Trade and Currencies: Economics and Politics", in J. Frankel (ed.), *The Regionalization of the World Economy*. Chicago: University of Chicago Press.

Fung, K.C, Hsiang-Chih Hwang, Francis Ng and Jesus Seade (2013). "International Trade and Production Networks: Comparisons of China and Greater China versus India and South Asia", *BOFIT Online 2013* No. 1. Helsinki: Bank of Finland, BOFIT-Institute for Economies in Transition.

Goldar, B. (2005). "Impact on India of Tariff and Quantitative Restrictions under WTO", *Working Paper* No. 172. New Delhi: ICRIER.

Grünfeld, Leo A. and Andres Moxnes (2003). "The Intangible Globalization: Explaining the Patterns of International Trade in Services", *Discussion Paper* No. 657. Norwegian Institute of International Affairs.

Harrigan, J. (1997), "Technology, Factor Supplies, and International Specialization: Estimating the Neo-classical Model", *American Economic Review* 87: 475-94.

Hillman, A.L. (1980). Observations on the Relation between 'Revealed Comparative Advantage' and Comparative Advantage as Indicated by Pre-trade Relative Prices", *Weltwirtschaftliches Archiv* 116(2): 315-21.

Helliwell, John F. (1996). "Do National Borders Matter for Quebec's Trade?", *Canadian Journal of Economics* 29(3): 507-22, August. Canadian Economics Association.

Helpman, Elhanan and Paul R. Krugman (1985). *Market Structure and Foreign Trade: Increasing Returns, Imperfect Competition, and the International Economy.* Cambridge: MIT Press

Hinloopen, J., and C. van Marrewijk (2001). "On the Empirical Distribution of the Balassa Index," *Review of World Economics/Weltwirtschaftliches Archiv* 137: 1-35.

Hirantha, Seekkuwa Wasam (2004). "From SAPTA to SAFTA: Gravity Analysis of South Asian Free Trade", Paper presented at the *European Trade Study Group (ETSG) Programme*. September. Nottingham.

Hoekman, Bernard and Alessandro Nicita (2011). "Trade Policy, Trade Costs, and Developing Country Trade", *World Development* 39(12): 2069-79. Elsevier.

Hummels, David and Peter J. Klenow (2005). "The Variety and Quality of a Nation's Exports", *American Economic Review*, June.

Iqbal, Ashiq (2012). "Non Tariff Barriers in South Asia, Addressing the Challenges", Presentation at a ArtNet/WTO Research Workshop on *Emerging Trade Issues in Asia and the Pacific: Meeting Contemporary Challenges*. Organized by ArtNet in Thailand. April.

Kee, Hiau Looi, Alessandro Nicita and Marcelo Olarreaga (2009). "Estimating Trade Restrictiveness Indices", *Economic Journal* 119: 172-99.

Kimura, Fukunari (2003). "Economic Analysis on Japan-Korea FTA: Services Trade". Manuscript. Keio University.

Kimura, F. and H. Lee (2004). "The Gravity Equation in International Trade in Services", *European Trade Study Group Conference*. University of Nottingham. 9-11 September.

Koopman, Robert, Zhi Wang and Shang-Jin Wei (2013). "The Value Added Structure of Gross Exports: Measuring Revealed Comparative Advantage by Domestic Content in Exports", *www.usitc.gov/research_and_analysis/*

Kowalski, Przemyslaw and Nora Dihel (2009). "India's Trade Integration, Realising the Potential", *OECD Trade Policy Working Paper* No. 88.

Krugman, Paul (1979). "Increasing Returns, Monopolistic Competition, and International Trade", *Journal of International Economics* 9: 469-79.

———. (2008). *The Increasing Returns Revolution in Trade and Geography*. Prize Lecture.

Kunimoto, K. (1977). "Typology of Trade Intensity Indices", *Hitotsubashi Journal of Economics* 17: 15-32

Lall, Sanjaya (2000). "The Technological Structure and Performance of Developing Country Manufactured Exports, 1985-98", *Oxford Development Studies* 28(3): 337-69.

Lall, Sanjaya and Manuel Albaladejo (2003). "China's Competitive Performance: A Threat to East Asian Manufactured Exports?", *Queen Elizabeth House Working Paper Series* 110.

Langhammer, Rolf J. (2004). "Revealed Comparative Advantages in the Services Trade of the United States, the European Union and Japan : What Do They Tell Us?", *The Journal of World Investment & Trade* 5(6): 887-96, ISSN 1660-7112.

Langhammer, Rolf J. and U. Heimenz (1990). *Regional Integration Among Developing Countries Opportunities Obstacles and Options*. Tubingen: Mohr.

Laursen, Keld (1998). "Revealed Comparative Advantage and the Alternatives as Measures of International Specialization", *Danish Research Unit for Industrial Dynamics DRUID Working Paper* No. 98-30. Copenhagen, Denmark.

Leromain, E. and Gianluca Orefice (2013). "New Revealed Comparative Advantage Index: Dataset and Empirical Distribution", *CEPII* No. 2013-20.

Linnemann, Hans (1966). *An Econometric Study of International Trade Flows*. Amsterdam, North Holland.

Long, Andrew G (2008). "Bilateral Trade in the Shadow of Armed Conflict", *International Studies Quarterly* 52: 81-101.

Manova, K. (2008). "Credit Constraints, Equity Market Liberalisations and International Trade", *Journal of International Economics* 76: 33-47.

Maskus, Keith E., Tsunehiro Otsuki and John S. Wilson (2005). "The Cost of Compliance with Product Standards for Firms in Developing Countries: An Econometric Study", *Policy Research Working Paper Series* 3590. The World Bank.

Matyas, L. (1997). "Proper Econometric Specification of the Gravity Model", *The World Economy* 20(3): 363-68.

———. (1998). "The Gravity Model: Some Econometric Considerations", *The World Economy* 21(3): 397-401.

McCallum, John (1995). "National Borders Matter: Canada-US Regional Trade Patterns", *The American Economic Review* 85(3): 615-23.

Mcmillan, Susan (1997). "Interdependence and Conflict", *Mershon International Studies Review*.

Micco, Alejandro, Ernesto Stein and Guillermo Ordonez (2003). "The Currency Union Effect on Trade: Early Evidence from EMU," *Economic Policy, CEPR & CES & MSH* 18(37): 315-56, October.

Mirza, Daniel and Giuseppe Nicoletti (2004). "What is So Special about Trade in Services?, *Research Paper* 2004/02. Leverhulme Centre for Research on Globalisation and Economic Policy

Moinuddin, Mustafa (2013). "Fulfilling the Promises of South Asian Integration: A Gravity Estimation", *ADBI Working Paper* 415.

Morrow, P. (2010), "Ricardian-Heckscher-Ohlin Comparative Advantage: Theory and Evidence", *Journal of International Economics* 82: 137-51.

Mukherjee, I.N. (2004). "Towards a Free Trade Area in South Asia: Charting a Feasible Course for Trade Liberalization with Reference to India's Role", *RIS Discussion Paper* No. 86. New Delhi: Research and Information Systems.

Nayar, Baldev R. (2006). "When Did the 'Hindu' Rate of Growth End?", *Economic and Political Weekly* 41(19): 1885-90 (May 13):

Noland, Marcus (2005). "Affinity and International Trade", *Working Paper Series* Number WP 05-3. Washington DC: Institute for International Economics.

Nunn, N. (2007), "Relationship-Specificity, Incomplete Contracts, and the Pattern of Trade", *Quarterly Journal of Economics* 122: 569-600.

Obstfeld, Maurice and Kenneth Rogoff (2000). "The Six Major Puzzles in International Economics: Is there a Common Cause?", *NBER Working Paper* 7777. Cambridge MA: National Bureau of Economic Research.

OECD (2002). *OECD Statistics on International Trade in Services, Detailed Tables by Partner Country 1999-2002'*

Okamoto, Yumiko (2006). *China and India: Challenges and Opportunities for ASEAN from Japanese Perspectives.* Kyoto, Japan: Dept. of Policy Studies, Doshisha University.

Plummer, Michael G. (2007). "Best Practices in Regional Trading Agreements: An Application to Asia", *The World Economy* 30(12): 1771-96.

Pöyhönen, P. (1963). "A Tentative Model for the Volume of Trade Between Countries", *Weltwirtschaftliches Archiv* 90: 93-99.

Pradhan, Samir Ranjan (2006). *India's Export Potential to the Gulf Cooperation Council Countries: A Gravity Model Analysis.* Asia Pacific Research and Training Network on Trade (ArtNet). Post Workshop Reports.

Rahman, M.M. (2003). "A Panel Data of Bangladesh's Trade: The Gravity Model Approach", Paper presented at the *European Trade Study Group (ETSG) 2003 Programme*. September. Madrid

Rahman, Mohammad Masudur, Chanwahn Kim and Laila Arjuman Ara (2013). "Enhancing Trade in Textile and Clothing in South Asia: The Role Trade Facilitation Can Play", *Global Trade and Customs Journal* 8(10). The Netherlands: Kluwer International BV.

Rahman, Mustafizur, Wasel Bin Shadat and Narayan Chandra Das (2006). *Trade Potential in SAFTA: An Application of Augmented Gravity Model.* Paper 61. Dhaka, Bangladesh: Centre for Policy Dialogue.

Rana, Pradumna B. and John Malcolm Dowling (2008). *South Asia: Rising to the Global Challenge.*

Raychaudhuri, Ajitava, Rajat Acharyya, Sugata Marjit, Debapriya Bhattacharya, Mustafizur Rahman and Manzur Alam Tipu (2003). "Trade Potentials of South Asian Economies Under the New Global Trade Regime: The Role of Some Non-Price Factors: A Case Study of India, Bangladesh and Sri Lanka", *SANEI Project Report* 2002-2003.

Reza, S. (1983). "Revealed Comparative advantage in the South Asian Manufacturing Sector: Some Estimates", *Indian Economic Journal* 31(2): 96-106.

Richardson, J.D. and C. Zhang (1999). "Revealing Comparative Advantage: Chaotic or Coherent Patterns across Time and Sector and US Trading Partner?", *NBER Working Paper* No. 7212.

Rodriguez-Delgado, J.D. (2007). "SAFTA: Living in a World of Regional Trade Agreements", *IMF Working Paper* 07/23.

Romalis, J. (2004), "Factor Proportions and the Structure of Commodity Trade", *American Economic Review* 94: 67-97.

Rose, Andrew. K. (2000). "One Money, One Market: Estimating the Effect of Common Currency on Trade", *Economic Policy* 15(30).

———. (2001). "Currency Unions and Trade: The Effect is Large," *Economic Policy* 33: 449-61.

———. (2003). "Does the WTO Make Trade More Stable?", *NBER Working Paper* No. 10207.

Schiff, Maurice and Alan L. Winters (2003). *Regional Integration and Development*. Washington DC: World Bank.

Shingal, Anirudh (2009). "Regional Trade Agreements and Services Trade" *mimeo, dev3.cepr.org/meets/wkcn/2/2404/papers/.*

Shinoj, P. and V.C. Mathur (2008). "Comparative Advantage of India in Agricultural Exports vis a vis Asia: A Post Reforms Analysis", *Agriculture Economics Research Review* 21: 60-66.

Shirotori, Miho and Ana Cristina Molina (2009). *South-South Trade: The Reality Check*. UNCTAD/DITC/TAB/2008/1. Geneva: UNCTAD.

Soloaga, Isidro and Alan L. Winters (1999). "How has Regionalism in the 1990s Affected Trade? *Policy Research Working Paper* 2156. Washington DC: World Bank.

Srinivasan, T.N. and G. Canonero (1993). *Preferential Trade Arrangement: Estimating the Effects on South Asia Countries*. Report, South-Asia Region. World Bank. September. pp.1-58

———. (1995). *Preferential Agreements in South Asia: Theory, Empirics and Policy*. Yale Growth Centre, Yale University.

Thakur, Devendra (2009). *Globalization and International Business*. Deep and Deep Publications.

Tharakan, P. K.M., I.V. Beveren and T.V. Ourti (2005). "Determinants of India's Software Exports and Goods Exports", *The Review of Economics and Statistics* 87(4): 776-80.

Tian, Wei and Miaoje Yu (2012). "China and India: Trends in Trade Over the Last Decade", *The Journal of China and Global Economics* 1(1): 27-38 (Spring).

Tinbergen Jan (1962). "An Analysis of World Trade Flows", in Jan Tinbergen (ed.), *Shaping the World Economy*. New York: The Twentieth Century Fund.

Tripathi, Sabyasachi and Nuno Carlos Leitão (2013). "India's Trade and Gravity Model: A Static and Dynamic Panel Data", *MPRA Paper* 45502.

Tumbarello, P. (2007). "Are Regional Trade Agreements in Asia Stumbling or Building Blocks? Implications for the Mekong-3 Countries", *IMF Working Paper* 07/53: 1-27.

Veeramani, C. (2008). "India and China: Changing Patterns of Comparative Advantage?" in R Radhakrishna (ed.), *India Development Report 2008*. New Delhi: Oxford University Press.

Veeramani, C. and Gordhan Kumar Saini (2011). "Impact of ASEAN-India Preferential Trade Agreement on Plantation Commodities: A Simulation Analysis", *Economic and Political Weekly*, XLVI: 83-92 (March 5).

Venables, Anthony J. (1999). *Regional Trade Agreements: A Force for Convergence or Divergence. elibrary.worldbank.org*

Viner, Jacob (1950). *The Customs Union Issue*. New York: Carnegie Endowment for International Peace.

Vollrath, T.L. (1987). "Revealed Competitive Advantage for Wheat", *Economic Research Service Staff Report* No. AGES861030. Washington DC: US Department of Agriculture.

———. (1989). "Competitiveness and Protection in World Agriculture", *Agricultural Information Bulletin* No. 567. Washington DC: Economic Research Service, US Department of Agriculture.

———. (1991). "A Theoretical Evaluation of Alternative Trade Intensity Measures of Revealed Comparative Advantage," *Weltwirtchaftliches Archiv* 127(2): 265-80.

Vollrath, T.L. and De Huu Vo (1990). "Agricultural Competitiveness in an Independent World" in *Agriclture and Governments in an Independent World. International Association of Agricultural Economists Occasional Paper* No. 5. Hampshire, England: Gower.

Walsh, Keith (2006). "Trade in Services: Does Gravity Hold? A Gravity Model Approach to Estimating Barriers to Services Trade", *The Institute for International Integration Studies Discussion Paper Series* No.iiisdp183.

Wei, Shang-Jin (2012). *Testimony before the U.S.-China Economics and Security Review Commission Hearing on the Evolving U.S.-China Trade and Investment Relationship.*

Wignaraja, Ganeshan (2011). "Economic Reforms, Regionalism and Exports: Comparing China and India", *Policy Studies* 60. Hawaii: East West Centre.

Williamson, John (2004). "A History of the Washington Consensus", Paper Commissioned by Fundacion CIDOB for a conference *From the Washington Consensus Towards a New Global Governance.* Barcelona. September 24-25.

Wilson, John S. and Tsunehiro Otsuki (2007). "Regional Integration in South Asia: What Role for Trade Facilitation?", *Policy Research Working Paper Series* 4423. Washington, DC: World Bank.

Wilson, John S., Catherine Mann and Tsunehiro Otsuki (2005). "Assessing the Benefits of Trade Facilitation: A Global Perspective", *World Economy* 28(6): 841-71.

Yeats, A.J. (1985). "On the Appropriate Interpretation of the Revealed Comparative Advantage Index: Implications of a Methodology based on Industry Sector Analysis", *Weltwirtschaftliches Archiv* 121(1): 61-73.

Yeaple, S. and S.S. Golub (2007). "International Productivity Differences, Infrastructure, and Comparative Advantage", *Review of International Economics* 15: 223-42.

Yu, Miaojie (2011). *Patterns of Trade, Comparative Advantage and Productivity in the ASEAN-China-India Region.* China Centre for Economic Research, Peking University. Available at: *http://ssrn.com/abstract=1854907*